ADIRONDACK HARD TIMES

Evolution of a Rich Man's Paradise

Andrew Egan, PhD

Published by The History Press
Charleston, SC
www.historypress.com

Copyright © 2021 by Andrew Egan
All rights reserved

Front cover, top: Keene Valley Public Library; *bottom*: Hotel Ampersand, 1907. Localwiki.org.
Back cover: Hamilton County Historian; *inset*: S.R. Stoddard, the New York Public Library.

First published 2021

Manufactured in the United States

ISBN 9781467148337

Library of Congress Control Number: 2021931149

Notice: The information in this book is true and complete to the best of our knowledge. It is offered without guarantee on the part of the author or The History Press. The author and The History Press disclaim all liability in connection with the use of this book.

All rights reserved. No part of this book may be reproduced or transmitted in any form whatsoever without prior written permission from the publisher except in the case of brief quotations embodied in critical articles and reviews.

To Andy, Ceil and Willa

CONTENTS

ACKNOWLEDGEMENTS

Adirondack Hard Times owes much to several astute observers of the Adirondack experience who have come before, especially Barbara McMartin, whose dispassionate reliance on the public record, rather than on emotion and hyperbole, guided her work. Libraries and historical societies scattered throughout the Adirondack Park, especially the Saranac Lake Free Library, the Goff-Nelson Memorial Library (Tupper Lake), the Lake Placid Public Library, the Keene Public Library, the Keene Valley Library, the Joan Weill Adirondack Library (Paul Smith's College) and the Hamilton County Historian, were indispensable repositories of information and images.

Adirondack Hard Times has also relied on reporting published in local and national newspapers, some long gone, to fill in historical gaps and provide news and perspectives related to the book's dominant themes. Most notable among the local papers are the *Adirondack Daily Enterprise*, *Tupper Lake Herald*, *Tupper Lake Free Press*, *Adirondack News*, *Lake Placid News*, *(Glens Falls) Post-Star*, *Albany Times Union* and *Malone Palladium*. Thanks to all the past and present editors and reporters of these and the many other newspapers that have kept the Adirondack story alive. A shout-out, too, to North Country Public Radio for its timely coverage of Adirondack issues.

Finally, many thanks to The History Press, especially to Banks Smither for effectively advocating for *Adirondack Hard Times* and to Rick Delaney and the rest of the editorial and art staff for helping to improve it. Thanks also to the editorial board of The History Press for expanding its library to include works that question prevailing norms and to my family and friends for allowing me the space to do the same.

INTRODUCTION

I didn't realize it then, but I began writing Adirondack Hard Times *in 1985, as I drove to the Adirondacks from New Hampshire, where I had been a student, then a logger and later a forester. I had never been to the Adirondacks before but imagined it to be like the bucolic and industrious northern New England that I was used to, just a little farther west.*

Driving across central New Hampshire, then Vermont, where my grandfather had a farm, I crossed Lake Champlain by ferry from Grand Isle in my red pickup, "Live Free or Die" hanging from the bumper, girlfriend and beagle in the seat next to me, hard hat, timber-marking gun, spare tire and assorted obligatory chains rattling around in the back. About to enter the Adirondack region, I was fully expecting to see simply a continuation of the same northern New England landscape when we disembarked. And why not? From east to west, it all looked pretty similar on a topographic map: green mountains and blue lakes and rivers punctuated by widely scattered rural communities.

Here's what I didn't know at the time:

In 1885, a forest preserve was created in northern New York, and seven years later, a "park" was established there, what is now the six-million-acre Adirondack Park, the boundaries of which were outlined on early maps with blue ink. It's not a park in the conventional sense, defined by the dictionary as a "piece of public land in or near a city that is kept free of houses and other buildings and can be used for pleasure and exercise" or, alternatively, as "a large area of public land kept in its natural state to protect plants and animals." Although the Adirondack Park is closer to the latter description, the place is too complex to reduce to a one-sentence dictionary definition.

First, it's not all public land. The Adirondack Park is mostly privately owned, although public ownership has been growing as a proportion of the Park's total area. And it's certainly not free of houses and buildings, since there are currently some 128,000 year-round residents living in 103 towns and villages scattered throughout the Park. Land use is controlled by layers of regulation and oversight. Designated as "forever wild," the 2.7 million acres of publicly owned and preserved forestland located inside the blue line are no longer available for harvesting, and forest management on private lands in the Park is subject to additional regulations not found elsewhere in the state.

It's also a place of extremes: stark natural beauty and teetering human ecosystems; blatant wealth and poignant rural poverty; and raw grassroots advocacy and polarized and polemicized political acrimony. Indeed, if you're an Adirondack local, you may be more likely to caustically contest that it's not a park at all—"a vast natural sanctuary," as the Adirondack Park Agency (APA), the region's managing authority, described the place on its website in 2020. It's where you live and work, where your kids were born and go to school, where generations of your ancestors once lived and are now buried. If you are a proponent of the Park, it's a place for outdoor recreation and wilderness solitude unequaled in the northeastern United States and for second-home owners seeking a tranquil retreat from the congestion of urban and suburban life. More recently, the Adirondacks also became a refuge from a global pandemic for those fleeing densely populated downstate New York, the epicenter for coronavirus infection and mortality during the spring of 2020.

The Adirondacks is also a whimsical place, where one Park observer described its landscape as looking like Bulgaria (compared to Vermont's Austria); where the most apparent lake in the village of Saranac Lake is Lake Flower and the most apparent lake in the village of Lake Placid is Mirror Lake; where a reputed early founder of the Park's forest preserve erased a couple of Adirondack mountain ecosystems then proposed to profit from building a railroad line into the Park's core (his proposal was rejected; after 150 years, the ecosystems are still recovering); where Long Lake Central School recently graduated just two students (in 2017, the Park contained seven of the ten smallest upstate New York school districts); and where the

Adirondacks' only daily newspaper proclaimed in its largest font of the summer of 2019—"It's River Pigs!"—the name of Tupper Lake's proposed professional baseball team, decided by a referendum that drew more voters than the town's school board elections.

Relying primarily on low-wage seasonal tourism and often unstable public-sector employment, the Park's mostly one-dimensional service economy lacks better-paying and more reliable, year-round employment in manufacturing, especially in forestry—once the backbone of economy and community in the Adirondacks—and the resilience and agility to adjust quickly to evolving social, economic and political realities.

The reasons for creating a northern forest preserve and then a larger park that contained that preserve were often controversial, generally driven by the special interests of a wealthy few but surreptitiously obscured by more populist slogans, usually beginning with the moral imperatives "save" and "protect." Nevertheless, many people today would agree that, at least conceptually, a park in northern New York wasn't such a bad idea. However, having doubled in size since its creation in 1892, the Adirondack Park now represents about one-fifth of the state's total land area, with little or no sense of a public land-acquisition endgame. Importantly for the region's local residents, those with mailing addresses outside the Adirondack Park own approximately 40 percent of all of the Park's residential parcels, a proportion that is growing as the Park's year-round population is declining and rapidly aging, graduating classes like the one at Long Lake Central School becoming more commonplace.

Several authors have attempted to chronicle a history of the Adirondacks, a goal that can be unexpectedly elusive. Perhaps the best known is a former banker and early transplant from New York City, Alfred Donaldson, whose two-volume *A History of the Adirondacks* was published in 1921. Donaldson offers a somewhat arrhythmic account of the Adirondacks and the creation of an Adirondack park, one that appears to suffer at times from a lack of objectivity and accountability. Nevertheless, his work has inevitably become a primary source for subsequent Adirondack narratives, leaving behind threads of historical ambiguity.

Of the many Adirondack historians and raconteurs, Barbara McMartin, the mathematician turned historian, has consistently sounded a critically discordant, yet relevant and well-researched, note. "It's not a model; it's a mess," McMartin asserted about the Park. Referring primarily to the Park's forest products sector, she wrote that the Adirondacks' "third world comparison is most telling with respect to exporting natural resources. The inability of third world countries to develop processing or manufacturing to boost the economic value of their products occurs right here. Too much of our resources are shipped out without benefitting local people." On the matter of trying to find some balance between preservation and economic and community development, she continued, "We have done a very good job of natural resource protection. We have done a very poor job of putting people in a natural setting….In the Adirondacks, where preservation is so advanced, very little has been done to place people in the natural areas in ways that protect those areas and enhance people's needs and desires to be part of nature." The impacts on local families and communities, although at times casually dismissed and coarsely rationalized by some as simply a function of life in rural America, have been pervasive. According to one observer of the Adirondack experience nearly a half century ago, the Adirondacks "is a depressed area, a part of Appalachia, with high rates of underemployment and unemployment and low per capita income." Data suggest that little has changed.

So, how did the Adirondack Park lose its way, at least according to some? In 1999, McMartin maintained that "the failures are all traceable to our bureaucracies. There are overlapping agencies, split regions, and multiple, competing governmental bodies. We in the Park are governed by entities that are parochial at every level. The only way that we are unique is in the mess that purports to govern our most precious resource and the people who need to live and work in it." The genesis of these failures, these bureaucracies, is more complex, however, evolving from a trail of often misrepresented Adirondack history and attempts by Gilded Age "sports" and their latter-day counterparts to carve out their version of a rich man's paradise in northern New York.

It is not the intent of this book to simply chronicle another Adirondack history. Nor is it the intent to either engage in or enflame existing tensions and polemics between some Adirondackers and the APA; among preservationists, conservationists and property-rights advocates; or between Adirondack locals and those "from away." Rather, *Adirondack Hard Times* is a story of local Adirondack realities: of struggling, remote mountain hamlets and government-dependent communities and of persistent rural poverty on a resource-rich landscape increasingly dominated by Adirondack great camps and second-home estates owned by influential interests from outside the Park. As a result, the Adirondack region has evolved into a geographic and political place often dominated by wealthy landowners who have been historically dependent on Adirondack locals while at the same time

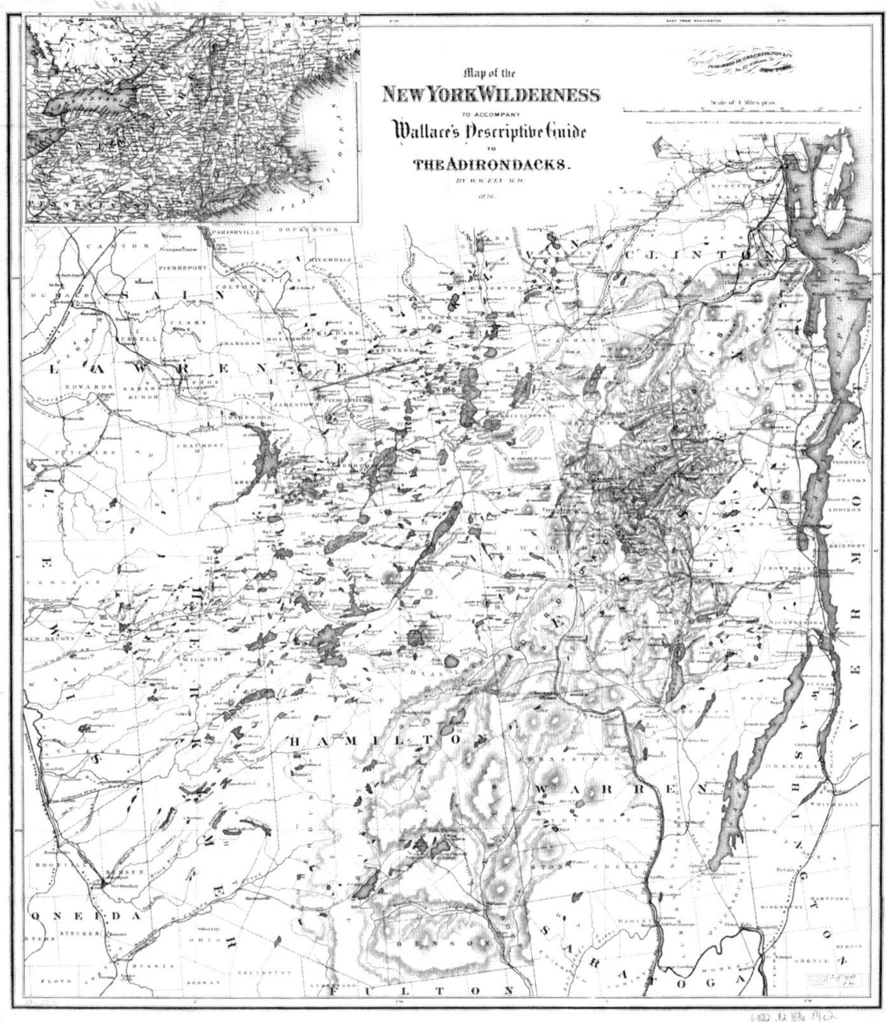

A forest preserve was created in this region in 1885, and seven years later, the Adirondack Park was established, outlined on maps with blue ink. *1876 map of the Adirondack region by W.W. Ely.*

appearing to keep them at arm's length so as not to compromise a distorted sense of quasi-self-sufficient wilderness adventurism.

Adirondack Hard Times stitches together scattered historical threads found in media reports and official state documents in an attempt to shape a more connected fabric, a more cohesive chronicle. In so doing, the aim is not so much to lend balance to the Adirondack historical record but rather to suggest a narrative that is built upon the best available data and contemporaneous media reportage. At its core, *Adirondack Hard Times* is a story of the evolution of a rich man's paradise—of the influence of wealth in the shaping of a region, its politics and its economy, often to the detriment of the human and natural ecosystems precariously positioned inside its blue line. It's also a story of history run amok, a narrative characterized by inconsistencies and contradictions, of the insidious effects of a follow-the-leader mentality among many Adirondack historians and storytellers, converting fantasy to truth merely by repeating it often enough—then using this "new truth" to form the basis of an often flawed and fabricated Adirondack ideal too often disguised as concern for the region's natural ecosystems.

Finally, *Adirondack Hard Times* serves as a note of caution—and perhaps also of hope—to other communities, regions, states and countries that may feel inspired by a utopian notion of a forever-wild place, "a model for the world," according to some, but have little or no appreciation for the day-to-day realities of life and livelihood inside a blue line.

> *A few minutes after rolling into the Park in that red pickup, for the first time observing the natural and human Adirondack ecosystems and communities as we passed through, my friend and I looked at each other in some astonishment, as if asking, "What happened here?"*
>
> Adirondack Hard Times *is one answer to that question.*

PART I

SHOOTING LOONS IN A THUNDERSTORM

The lands of the state, now owned or hereafter acquired, constituting the forest preserve as now fixed by law, shall be forever kept as wild forest lands. They shall not be leased, sold, or exchanged, or be taken by any corporation, public or private, nor shall the timber thereon be sold, removed or destroyed.
—Article XIV of the New York State Constitution, 1894

Despite success in the preservation arena…the description of today's Adirondacks includes government subsidy dependence, low incomes, high unemployment, low-wage jobs, and a declining manufacturing base.
—Erickson, "In Search of Sustainable Development"

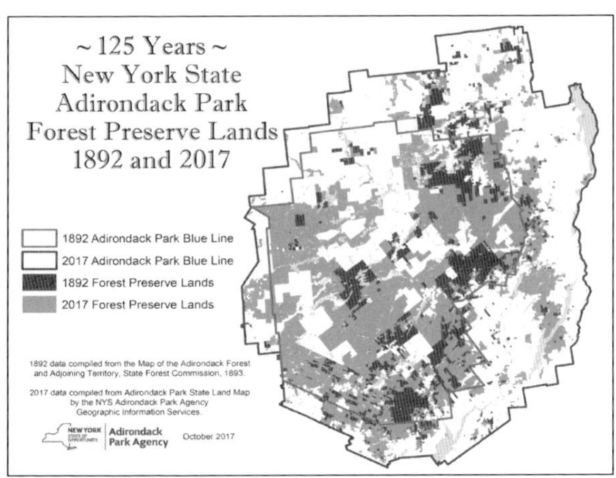

A 2017 map of the Adirondack Park, showing the location of forest preserve lands within its blue line. *Adirondack Park Agency.*

1
NABOBS AND NIMRODS

Boatloads of jolly campers and sportsmen, with their guides and outing impedimenta, were constantly passing and repassing along the principal waterways, which in those days were the only avenues of communication leading towards the choicest sporting sections of the Woods. The carries and trails were thronged.
—"Adirondack" Harry Radford, 1905[1]

Much of the history of the Adirondacks and the Adirondack Park is built on the often contradictory writings and inconsistent behaviors of several historical figures—men who are said to have been champions of a forever-wild Adirondack wilderness. Three characters in particular stand out as among the most often celebrated early advocates for wilderness adventurism, preservation and, ultimately, an Adirondack park. However, as with much of Adirondack history, it's more complicated than that. Of these putative Adirondack icons, one left behind a confusing legacy of ramblings and misadventures that are inconsistent with any notion of natural resource conservation or preservation; another handed down a culture that encouraged mass tourism, poor sportsmanship and lasting damage to mountain and aquatic ecosystems; and the last bequeathed a legacy of privileged and poorly informed environmentalism. In their own way, all contributed to the evolution of a rich man's paradise in northern New York.

Uncooperative Wilderness Icon

In its online history of the Adirondack Park, the Adirondack Park Agency (APA) cites testimony from Verplanck Colvin, awkwardly described by the New York State Department of Environmental Conservation (DEC) as "the almost legendary Adirondack surveyor." According to the APA's website in 2020, Colvin supported "the creation of an Adirondack Park or timber preserve" before the New York State legislature in 1874. Eleven years later, Colvin's testimony persuaded the state to create a forever-wild forest preserve. Quoting Colvin, the APA wrote: "Unless the region be preserved essentially in its present wilderness condition, the ruthless burning and destruction of the forest will slowly, year after year, creep onward."

Colvin failed to acknowledge, or was unaware, that the fires to which he alluded were most likely caused by either the burning of fallows by farmers or the carelessness of recreationists who had begun to flock to the Adirondacks from the urban northeastern United States. Some 150 years after Colvin's testimony, the Adirondack Regional Tourism Council cited Colvin as a founder of the Adirondack Park, stating on its 2020 website: "Clearcutting was a growing concern for many in the late 1800s." Giving credit to Colvin for raising "awareness for the need to create a Forest Preserve," the council asserted that, in 1870, "Colvin recorded his first ascent of Seward Mountain—where he witnessed the widespread devastation of the logging industry." Consistent with assertions of many observers of the Adirondack experience, this placed blame for forest destruction and devastation squarely on loggers, despite widely available records that suggest otherwise. Indeed, state reports tell us that only scattered trees were being harvested for lumber during that period.

There were other inconsistencies around Colvin's sense of forest destruction in the Adirondacks. For example, his earlier ascent of Seward Mountain was significant enough to have been reported in the *New York Times* on November 21, 1870, under the title "The Adirondack Region—Ascent of Mount Seward." According to one account, Colvin climbed the 4,347-foot Seward Mountain in Franklin County in 1870 and "saw the extensive damage being done by lumbermen in the Adirondacks." As an Albany-born lawyer, initially with little or no prior backcountry experience, it's reasonable to wonder whether Colvin would have been able to distinguish commercial logging from the cultural practices of farmers. To confound matters, another quote attributed to Colvin while on Seward, proclaimed the wild, pristine nature of what he saw: "Wilderness everywhere, lake on lake, river on river,

Verplanck Colvin, 1897. Colvin was an "almost legendary" Adirondack surveyor and an uncooperative icon of advocates for a forever-wild forest preserve in the Adirondacks. *Lake Placid Public Library*.

mountain on mountain, numberless." Colvin's description was supported by the First Annual Report of the Forest Commission of the State of New York for the year 1885: "With but little exception, [the Adirondack region] is an unbroken wilderness…containing over 4,000,000 acres, of which the State has acquired title to over 800,000 acres." During his climb, did Colvin witness extensive logging damage, the creation and management of fallows or wilderness everywhere from his perch on Seward?

As has occurred repeatedly in various Adirondack histories, Colvin failed to recognize that forest fires during this time, and to which he alluded, were not directly related to the logging slash that was a byproduct of timber harvesting. Halting the selective removal of spruce on an Adirondack forest preserve, for example, would have had little or no impact on the proliferation of large, clear-cut fallows and the forest fires that farmers carelessly created when fallow fires escaped. As for Colvin's contentions about who or what was to blame for forest destruction, there is this irony from the *Enterprise* in 2004: "A fire started by Verplanck Colvin and his surveying team in 1876 on top of St. Regis Mountain became out of control, destroying most of the summit and leaving it bare." For Colvin and his surveying crew, this was not an isolated incident. Where plant communities have not been able to restore themselves naturally after Colvin's clear-cutting, burning and subsequent soil erosion, fragile mountaintop ecosystems have been lost. Colvin could not get away with some of his surveying antics under the forever-wild clause for which it is claimed he was a proponent.

Culpability for forest destruction aside, Colvin's position on wilderness and forest preservation is a bit murkier than that offered by either the APA's or the council's abbreviated and selective versions of Adirondack history. It's debatable whether Colvin was a consistent advocate of wilderness protection, or if he, like many of his contemporaries, was more of an opportunist and advocate for other interests, including the exploitation of the Adirondack region. Colvin, for example, was behind the proposed New York, Canadian

Pacific Railroad that was to compete with the New York Central, which had already established itself in the Adirondack region. Colvin's proposed rail line would have originated in Albany and cut through Fulton County and the Adirondacks on its way to Ogdensburg. The application was ultimately denied by the state in 1902. Pointing out Colvin's hypocrisy on the matter, the *Gloversville Daily Leader* reported on October 4 of that year that "Col. Ashley W. Cole, president of the state [railroad] commission, stated to President Verplanck Colvin that it was well known to be the state's policy to refuse to permit any further railroad construction through the Adirondacks. He recalled to Mr. Colvin that he had himself been strenuous in advocating this policy when a few years ago he had been at the head of the Adirondack State land survey."

Despite his "almost legendary" status among today's Adirondack icons, during Colvin's time, not everyone viewed him as such or supported his work, seeing him more as an opportunist than an intrepid explorer, consistent with his failed attempt to extend another rail line into the Adirondacks. As reported in the *Ithaca Daily Journal* in 1880, while Colvin was still surveying the Adirondacks: "Albany papers announce that Verplanck Colvin has suspended his Adirondack survey for this season, but will be ready to commence operations next year. We suppose in the mean time [*sic*] he will survey the state treasury and draw therefrom a good many thousand dollars for services which may appear very valuable to V.C., but which are not appreciated by taxpayers." The *Journal*'s reporting suggests a couple of things about Colvin in 1880: He and his Adirondack survey work were reasonably well known in the state, and he was neither widely revered nor his work highly regarded by some in the media.

His critics were right to be skeptical, given subsequent reports of his careless surveying work—which may have also explained the discrepancies between Colvin's largely discredited claims of forest destruction by logging and actual conditions on the ground. In a profession that demands attention to detail, Colvin was not known for careful record keeping, with many of his surveys containing considerable errors. According to the early Adirondack historian Donaldson, a contemporary of Colvin: "The years have shown his work as a whole to be of very uneven scientific value. The resurvey of many of his lines has proven them to be inaccurate. Much of the great mass of material which he collected, owing to the lack of systematic filing, tabulation, or indexing, was made useless to his successors. His office in Albany, indeed, looked more like the dressing-room of a sporting-club than the repository of valuable records." Adding insult to injury, according to Colvin's Adirondack guides, "he was neither a good woodsman nor a good manager." That he was not considered a capable woodsman is not too surprising, given his background as a city lawyer turned self-made surveyor, for whom mapping the wilderness was originally a hobby.

Significantly for the future of an Adirondack park, Colvin's position on establishing an Adirondack forest preserve does not appear to be as clear-cut as has been depicted by either popular history or the APA. Colvin appeared to be more of an advocate for a timber reserve than for a forever-wild forest preserve, although his views on this have been confusing. A report in the *Watertown Re-Union* in 1876 quoted Colvin: "This Park should be guarded, that it may furnish a supply of lumber when other resources shall have failed." His words described a timber reserve, not a forever-wild forest preserve, as it was later interpreted. He continued: "The governments of Europe have given us an example in that direction which might be well followed. Let our own Empire State be the first in the Union to appreciate the importance of prudently utilizing and preserving there [*sic*] vast resources of water power and supplies of lumber." Again, this is a timber reserve concept, based on the prudent utilization rather than the outright preservation of timber grown on public lands. During the period, the terms *reserve* and *preserve* were sometimes used interchangeably, typically describing the sustainable management and utilization of forests for timber. Indeed, the Second Annual Report of the Forest Commission of the State of New York for the year 1886 states that the preservation of forests is essential first "for the value of the timber, both present and future. With our rapidly growing population the demand for timber is daily increasing, while the supply is rapidly decreasing."

At the same time, Colvin appeared to support the creation of a wilderness resort, a rich man's paradise: "This great wilderness region should be preserved in its primal condition, so as to afford the people of this and the eastern States an accessible resort where they may find genuine field sports." The notion of a preserve, a "resort" in "primal condition," more clearly aligns Colvin with both a forever-wild preserve concept, as well as with the period's upper class, those who could afford to enjoy the Adirondacks as an "accessible resort." In 1876, virtually the only people wealthy enough to be engaging in "field sports" in Adirondack resorts were a rather pampered cohort of urban sportsmen with questionable wilderness and hunting ethics. The carelessness of participants in the very field sports for which Colvin was advocating was, along with farmers and locomotives, among the major threats to Adirondack ecosystems, as we'll see later. Yet despite these inconsistencies and Colvin's own hypocritical behavior, the commissioner of New York State's DEC, in a guest commentary published in the May 30, 2017 issue of the *Adirondack Daily Enterprise*, just beneath a graphic showing the results of a web poll asking "Should residents of Lake Placid and the surrounding area be allowed to keep chickens" (chickens prevailed, with 82 percent—of voters, not chickens—in favor), praised Colvin's determination as pivotal to the creation of the Adirondack Park.

There is little doubt that Colvin made contributions to an early, albeit at times rather careless, sense of Adirondack geography and spirit of wilderness adventurism. However, fading into obscurity later in life, the man who in modern times has been prematurely beatified as an Adirondack surveying legend and the Adirondacks' best friend was destined to become a recluse on the streets of Albany, passing away in an asylum in 1920 at the age of seventy-three. Tellingly, Colvin's obituary as published in the *Elizabethtown Post* that year, while describing him as an Adirondack surveyor and for having shot and killed a mountain lion (an act for which he was, according to some accounts, nicknamed "The Panther"), makes no mention of him as an advocate for the establishment of a forest preserve or an Adirondack park, both of which, by the time of his death, had been in existence for more than a quarter century. In the end, history suggests that the enigmatic Colvin was neither a consistently competent surveyor nor a clear and consistent advocate for Adirondack wilderness, despite assertions by those searching for an Adirondack icon to whom to tether their advocacy for a forever-wild Adirondacks and a rich man's resort. Nevertheless, despite Colvin's wobbly legacy and his unsettled support for a forest preserve, forever-wild advocates have continued to hold him up as an Adirondack wilderness icon, cutting, pasting and interpreting his words and actions so selectively as to compromise the historical record.

But Colvin was a contemporary of another, even more elusive, character, a preacher whose story was so compelling to many and his role in the development of a forever-wild rich man's paradise so significant that he was ordained during his lifetime with the honorary prenomen "Adirondack."

Prodigal Wanderer

Perhaps no one personifies the disconnect between Adirondack mythology and reality better than William "Adirondack" Murray. Like Colvin, not only was he an enigma while alive, but local Adirondack historians and storytellers have often whitewashed his past in an attempt to contrive another elusive icon for the early Adirondack experience. Over the years, headlines in Adirondack newspapers have hailed Murray as an Adirondack icon, a friend of wilderness guides, a preacher of the gospel of the wilderness and an Adirondack pied piper. Referring to Murray as a "hero," a writer for the *Lake Placid News* asserted in 1985 that the "existence of so much accessible wilderness in our back yard is due in large measure to two men: William Henry Harrison Murray and Verplanck Colvin." We've discussed Colvin and his enigmatic, and at times contradictory, sense of wilderness preservation. But what of Murray as Adirondack icon and hero? And what is his relevance to today's Adirondack Park?

A contemporary of Colvin, Murray was born in Guilford, Connecticut, in 1840, on the same day that William Henry Harrison was elected president of the United States. He was thus named for the president, though Murray was more likely to use the initials W.H.H. than his full name. A poor student, he nevertheless graduated from Yale in 1862. Murray made his first trips to the Adirondacks in 1866, staying "a couple of months in the summer time, accompanied by his family, in the wilderness of the 'North Wood' living the life of a hunter and fisher, with all the means and appliances for taking deer and trout," according to the *Malone Palladium* in 1869. Murray moved from Connecticut to Boston in 1868, six months later publishing his influential book *Adventures in the Wilderness*.[2] He was among the first to write about the Adirondacks and his experiences there, including his assertion that he hooked three trout with a single cast. In his book, Murray described the Adirondack wilderness as located "between the Lake George and Champlain on the east, and the river St. Lawrence on the north and west. It reaches northward as far as the Canada line, and southward to Booneville." However, despite the title of his book, there is little about his life that would suggest that Murray was very intrepid.

Indeed, it's difficult to glean from his writings what Murray truly believed, so itinerant and meandering was his walk through life. Not unlike his journey, Murray's *Adventures in the Wilderness* is liberally punctuated by disconnects, bluster and evasion. For example, describing his sense of adventure and sportsmanship and his aversion to hiking through the woods, Murray wrote: "If there is one kind of work which I detest more than another, it is tramping; and, above all, tramping through a lumbered district. How the thorns lacerate you! How the brambles tear your clothes and pierce your flesh! How the meshwork of fallen tree-tops entangles you!" Given the very scattered removal of large spruce trees that characterized Adirondack

W.H.H. "Adirondack" Murray, 1875. Murray's book *Adventures in the Wilderness* inspired droves of "sports" and other wealthy tourists, known to some as Murray's Fools, to throng to the Adirondacks for a pampered wilderness experience. *From Radford's 1905* Adirondack Murray, a Biographical Appreciation, *Library of Congress.*

logging at the time, it is just as likely that, if Murray was describing tramping in the Adirondacks, these weren't "lumbered districts," but rather clearings created by early Adirondack farmers and homesteaders. Describing his pampered Adirondack backcountry experience, he continued: "Now in the North Woods, owing to their marvelous water-communication, you do all your sporting from your boat. If you wish to go one or ten miles for a 'fish,' your guide paddles you to the spot, and serves you while you handle the rod. This takes from recreation every trace of toil. You have all the excitement of sporting, without any attending physical weariness….I have sported a month at a time, without walking as many miles as there are weeks in the month."

Murray described his Adirondack exploits with considerable hyperbole and bravado, much of which would appeal to the imagination of an unsuspecting, wealthy, urban public curious but naive about northern New York's wilderness. This was America's Gilded Age, a time when industrialization, the economy and leisure were growing rapidly, forming an elite social and economic class of chronically overprivileged, concentrated wealth that masked high rates of urban poverty and discrimination, especially against disadvantaged post–Civil War African Americans and often destitute European immigrants. The resulting disparity in wealth contributed to a period during which political processes and influence were controlled by the few who possessed the means to seek out their own sense of adventure in New York's newly rediscovered northern wilderness while ultimately carving out and protecting their own claims to a rich man's paradise.

His book's hyperbole aside, it's questionable whether Murray's *Adventures in the Wilderness* was a truly original work or simply uncited scroungings from the earlier work of the then clergyman, author and Adirondack rambler Joel T. Headley,[3] from whom he appears to have liberally borrowed. For example, compare this 1849 account by Headley with Murray's, published almost twenty years later: "Thinking he had heard rifle shots, Headley was corrected by his Indian guide: 'What were they then?' I inquired. 'Trees,' he replied. 'But,' said I, 'there is not a breath of air this morning, while it blew very hard yesterday afternoon.' 'They always fall,' he replied, 'before a storm—it will storm to-morrow.'"

Now Murray in 1869 (p. 104), hearing a similar noise, "a muffled roar, filling the air," and being advised by his guide, John Plumbley, as to its meaning: "'Yes,' said John, as the noise died away,—'yes, it *will* rain. The old trees never lie. Those sounds you have just heard are made by falling trees. You always hear them before a storm.' 'But, John,' I exclaimed, 'what makes them fall this morning? There is not a breath of air stirring?'"

In addition, like Headley before him, Murray describes an "apparition" at Phantom Falls, believed by some to be Headley's Raquette Falls. Headley also devotes almost an entire chapter to hunting deer with jacklights; coincidentally, so does Murray. It would seem unlikely that similarities in these two narratives, written some twenty years apart, were accidental.

Failing to be of any genuine historical value, Murray's book was essentially a field guide to early Adirondack tourism that had been criticized by the *Lake Placid News* in 1926 as a "grossly exaggerated account of the region." Consistent with his love of fishing and hunting, Murray's primary interest in writing his book was the rather self-serving preservation of the Adirondack wilderness for the benefit of urban sports—a contradictory juxtaposition that pits precepts of wilderness preservation against the more utilitarian values of a small but wealthy cohort of tourists and "sports," who, influenced by Murray, were beginning to view the Adirondacks as their private playground.

Joel T. Headley, clergyman, author, Adirondack rambler and, later, New York secretary of state. Headley published *The Adirondack; or Life in the Woods* in 1849. *Internet archives, The Miscellaneous Works of the Rev. J.T. Headley.*

In his book, Murray describes rather civilized scenes of lean-tos and burning campfires, built and attended to by well-paid guides, reflecting the pampered treatment of nineteenth-century Adirondack sportsmen while presaging ominous harbingers of what was about to come for the region: overfishing that threatened native fish stocks as early as the nineteenth century; forest trails jammed with fashionably attired would-be adventurers; and the catastrophic wildfires of the late nineteenth and early twentieth centuries, many of them caused by careless tourists and sportsmen. Indeed, in 1877, just eight years after the publication of his book, Murray himself complained: "I have not put my fly rod together four times in four years. The Adirondack waters will have to be stocked by artificial means before a fly rod is needed on them and it will take six years to do it." This is a rather selfish lament, to which William Chapman White,[4] *New York Times* columnist and author of *Adirondack Country*, observed some decades later: "I fully agree with Murray but much of it is due to overdrawn descriptions in Murray's own writings" that encouraged a mass invasion of wealthy and careless tourists—"Murray's Fools," as they had come to be known—who possessed little or no real appreciation for conservation, drawn to the Adirondacks by Murray's own romantic mythology and contorted sense of adventure and sportsmanship. Referring to the Adirondacks, White asserted in 1954 that "no area in America has had a more miserable story of ruthless squandering of natural resources…based on the supposition that the stock of fish and game, as well as trees, was infinite."

Another view of Murray and his adventures suggested that "his hunting and fishing tall tales, together with promises of improved health, caused the greatest invasion of the north woods ever witnessed by resort hotels. Accommodations were stretched to the breaking point with some guests (or so the story goes) being forced to sleep on billiard tables. On a rainy summer day, Martin[5] returned from a fishing expedition to find his lobby overrun with a swarm of Murray's Fools, loudly clamoring for rooms as his wife was attempting to register them," according to a 1986 story in the *Adirondack Daily Enterprise*.

It is doubtful that Murray experienced many genuine backcountry adventures in the Adirondacks—certainly none that drew on his self-reliance. Indeed, the print media of the period seemed to be on to him. Appearing to put Murray in his place, in 1871, the *Brooklyn Eagle* described him as having acquired fame as "a sensational summer tourist" rather than as an intrepid sportsman and adventurer. Murray seemed better versed at describing what Adirondack tourists should wear than how to survive in the north country's wilderness. His book included "full lists of articles needed, both by ladies and gentlemen, for an outfit," according to the *Malone Palladium* in 1869. The result was a decidedly tame Adirondack experience, one that avoided the discomforts of the backcountry. Referring to one of his excursions into the Adirondack wilderness, in 1875, the *Daily Journal* of Ogdensburg mockingly observed that "Adirondack Murray and a party of Bostonians returned home today from a four weeks sojourn in the North Woods. The flies drove them out." Despite achieving status as an

Adirondack icon—at least among armchair adventurers and some latter-day wilderness raconteurs—through his writing, Murray inadvertently helped solidify his own reputation for backcountry deception. Describing his propensity for making things up on the fly, in 1887 the *Sun* wrote about "the Rev. Adirondack Murray, whose specialty is fish stories." It appeared that excursions to the Adirondacks by Murray and his followers were as much for show and bragging rights as they were for anything approaching a true wilderness experience. Yet these pseudo-adventurers would ultimately help to form a foundation for sympathy and political support for the creation of a rich man's paradise.

Eventually, life began to unravel for Murray, as he accumulated debt to creditors in Boston and New Haven that he couldn't pay. An extensive page-one article in the *Sun* in 1879 traced some of the troubles: "The Rev. William H.H. Murray's business troubles have caused no surprise in Guilford…almost everyone you meet here says that he knew the parson would go to pieces sooner or later." According to some people in Guilford, Murray's father was a bit of a ne'er-do-well and teller of tall tales, and, as it turns out, his son wasn't far behind. "He could talk very big, too…and that's where the boy got his gift of talking," according to a local farmer. Writing of Murray's lack of wilderness experience and veracity, the *Sun* continued:

> *Somebody induced him to go into the then almost unknown Adirondack region one summer about ten years ago. He was gone a month and thereabouts, and came back a wildly excited man over what he called the glorious sport to be found there.… There appeared a book said to have been written by an orthodox clergyman, entitled Adventures in the Wilderness. The stories that were told were so incredible that the clergyman was charged with exaggeration.… When his friends asked him if his marvelous stories of the Adirondack region were true he always told them to try it for themselves and see.*

What of Murray and the creation of a park in the Adirondacks, a forever-wild retreat for the few who could afford to take advantage of it? Apart from his rants against "lumbermen," Murray's writings supported a gentrified wilderness experience disguised as backcountry adventurism that catered to the perverted sportsmanship engaged in by many of the period's urban elites. But during Murray's time, attitudes about backcountry customs and values were changing, as outlined in this

1874 report from the *Daily Journal*, which didn't hesitate to take a shot at Murray and his followers:

> *The hunting and fishing and scenery of the Adirondack wilderness may not be in peril, but, as we have been able to gather the traditions of that region, one of the principal adjuncts to enjoyment there is in peril. The question of establishing the Adirondack park has again been under consideration in the Assembly, and from the debate it would appear that the business of civilizing the wilderness is to be carried to a point likely to interfere with the common law rights of venerable sportsmen, who have been accustomed to revive their failing energies in the region for the last quarter of a century or more. The Rev. Adirondack Murray, and his disciples, brought much scandal upon those virtuous woods, and others have perverted their use from that of recreation to sensational book writing and lecturing.*

Through their contorted backcountry antics and attitudes and bumptious storytelling, Murray and his followers were seen as compromising the inherent wilderness values of the Adirondacks—self-reliance, natural-resource stewardship and respect for ecosystem integrity—including by the print media of the period.

Adirondack Murray died on March 3, 1904, at the age of sixty-four at his home in Guilford in the same room in which he was born. Under the headline "'Adirondack' Murray Dead," the *Sun* described him as "a preacher, a racehorse owner, and author," foregoing descriptions of the more sordid aspects of his prodigal life. It can be argued that Adirondack Murray and his adventures and misadventures are early manifestations of the disconnect between the romanticist's and the realist's take on life in the Adirondacks, between the tall tales spun by raconteurs and the well-researched and objective interpretations offered by too few of the region's more dispassionate observers. While this may seem harmless enough on the surface, this history interpreted and passed down as fact has helped inform the foundation of institutions, policies and public opinion related to the Adirondack experience and the Adirondack Park experiment, sometimes with unintended consequences and misinformed, yet all too durable, outcomes.

An Adirondack icon who will be remembered as long as there is an Adirondack history. A friend of backcountry guides. A preacher of the gospel of wilderness. Adirondack pied piper. Adirondack hero. These are among the descriptions of Murray offered by Adirondack historians. Given his checkered history, it is difficult to imagine him as the respected author, devoted preacher, and rugged adventurer that his adoring biographer—the other "Adirondack"—and subsequent others have made him out to be.

"Nonsensical Bear Twaddle"

While not quite the historical figure that Colvin and Murray were, it would be an omission to ignore the personage who came to be known as Adirondack Harry, since a few modern-day raconteurs ascribe at least some value to his contributions to the conservation of the Adirondacks and to our appreciation of Adirondack history and the region's iconic figures, especially Murray. Moreover, in addition to also being honored with the prenomen "Adirondack," Harry Radford was among a litany of misinformed writers and pseudo-adventurers who laid the historical groundwork for an Adirondack park and a rich man's paradise in northern New York.

Harry Radford was born in 1880 in New York City and remained there long enough to earn an engineering degree from Manhattan College. Reports related to Radford often referred to him as Adirondack Harry, Murray's second coming. But, like Murray, Radford was a relative novice when it came to the Adirondacks, with history suggesting that he was either a visionary conservationist or poorly informed environmentalist. A New York City journalist, Radford was publisher and editor of *Woods and Waters* and founded the Association of New York Sportsmen in 1901. In 1900, he moved to the Adirondack hamlet of North Creek, then the northern terminus of the Adirondack Railway. Ironically, perhaps Radford's most deliberate attempt to demonstrate his command of the wilderness and his dominance over the people who inhabited it resulted in his death at the young age of thirty-two.

Much can be learned about Radford from his biography of Adirondack Murray. According to Donaldson, Adirondack Harry "was an avowed apostle" of Murray's, "whom he admired to the point of adoration," accurately observing that Radford's rambling 1905 *Biographical Appreciation* of Murray contained "much more appreciation than biography." "When he came to write his biographical sketch, he not only had nothing new to offer, but he also seemed ignorant of much that was common knowledge concerning Murray's early life." Indeed, Radford's meandering tribute to Murray embodied one of several early disconnects between romantic and more realistic renditions of Adirondack life and the characters who inhabited it, leading to a fragile thread of Adirondack mythology that has persisted into the twenty-first century.

Perhaps not too surprisingly, none of Murray's transgressions show up in Radford's rather shallow authorized biography of his friend and mentor. Instead, despite much that had been written to the contrary, Radford described Murray as "one of the few great sportsmen America has produced." According to Radford, "Mr. Murray himself had expressed the desire that I should be his biographer"—not surprising, since many of the writers of the time appeared to have grown weary of Murray's antics and self-adulation. But not Radford. Of his questionable business exploits, Radford observed: "Mr. Murray's career was a shining example of a 'self-made man'—of the rise of an [*sic*] humble New England farmer lad into worldly prominence and worth." No mention is made of Murray's bankruptcy or of being on the run from creditors, as was widely reported by the media of the period.

Regarding arguments over whether Murray was conveying accurate depictions of actual events or tall tales in *Adventures in the Wilderness*, Radford curiously asserted that "the little book…was not a cruel hoax, but a truthful revelation." As an example of how out of touch he was, Radford rather carelessly claimed that Murray "was the greatest of all American orators" at a time when the likes of Frederick Douglass, Ralph Waldo Emerson, William Jennings Bryant and Abraham Lincoln were using words to make truly significant and lasting impressions that shaped late nineteenth- and early twentieth-century American society. Murray's oratory of self-promotion and deception came nowhere close to this level of influence—revealing more about Radford and his infatuation with Murray than about Murray himself.

Radford also described Murray as "the most competent sportsman of his day," despite newspaper accounts of Murray's hunting antics and questionable sense of sportsmanship. In addition, Radford's book was published during a time of some furor over the ethics of deer-jacking and hounding, calling into question both Radford's and Murray's senses of sportsmanship and wildlife conservation. For example, by this time, deer-jacking, described in detail and popularized by Murray in his *Adventures in the Wilderness*, was illegal in New York, the practice's lack of sportsmanship and its negative impact on the region's deer herds having been questioned for some years prior to the publication of Radford's rather adoring, but decidedly bland and tedious, biography of Murray.

Radford, ostensibly a staunch conservationist who was instrumental in bringing attention to dwindling moose, elk, black bear and beaver populations in the Adirondacks, was in favor of state ownership of all lands in the Adirondack Park, stating that "the wisest thing the state could possibly do would be to immediately acquire the entire park area," according to the *Malone Farmer* in 1904. Radford offered no solution to the mass relocation of the area's permanent residents that that would imply, much less the disposition of his own home in North Creek, located inside the Park's blue line. An inexperienced and idealistic city dweller with a naive and self-serving sense of conservation, Radford was described as being out of touch with backcountry values, local Adirondack communities and their economies and commonsense wildlife management.

Adirondack Radford was also thought by some to be disingenuous in his motivations to restore certain wildlife species to the Adirondacks. He was accused by the local media of "four-flushing," described by the *Elizabethtown Post* in 1904 as an "evil" that involves "the passing of ostensibly altruistic or beneficent legislation for the sake of having one's name connected with it." Radford's proposed bear conservation legislation, for example, was criticized in the *Post* article as "the self-aggrandizement of a clever city boy endowed with enough self-conceit to picture himself posing for a life-size painting, one hand on the breast of a frock coat, the other resting on the back of a bear licking his feet and labeled 'Radford the Emancipator of Bruin' or 'Lincoln of the Black Bear.'" The *Post* further described Radford as having only "passed months" in the Adirondacks, while the author of the article had "passed years hunting and fishing in the Adirondacks," calling into question the would-be conservationist's authenticity. Nevertheless, despite questions about his motivations, Radford was credited with the reintroduction of populations of beaver, moose and elk and protections for the black bear population. It appears that his heart may have been in the right place, descriptions of Radford as a "four-flusher" and out-of-touch environmentalist notwithstanding.

From what one can discern from reportage of the period, Radford's sense of wildlife management—whether well intentioned or not—was surely misinformed and his appreciation of Adirondack culture and customs nearly nonexistent. For example, Radford's proposed legislation to protect Adirondack black bear populations was caustically described by the *Elizabethtown Post* in 1904 as "nonsensical bear twaddle." Critical of his lack of experience with the Adirondacks and its rural culture, the *Post* said of Radford: "a young fellow barely 23 years of age who was born and brought up in the city and who has had 19 years in the woods must have been *remarkably precocious*," having ventured "into the country a few days in summer time," vaguely reminiscent of criticisms of Murray's rather limited Adirondack experiences. The crux of the controversy was the damage being wrought by bear on Adirondack sheep herds and Radford's apparent lack of appreciation of the concerns of local sheep farmers. The article continued, "Bruin dens up about six months of the year and the city enthusiast [i.e., Radford] would protect him for three months—July, August and September—just when he does the most damage."

Radford's attempt to reestablish moose populations in the Adirondacks was also criticized for its naivete about wildlife management and moose behavior. According to a story in the *North Creek News Enterprise* in 1967, "Radford's attempt to restock the moose—while made in good faith—was aborive [*sic*] for two reasons—the first was the moose were migratory in the extreme and soon took off for the North Country from which they came. The second reason was that the animals were liberated on arrival instead of being kept under fence until the first crop of calves were [*sic*] born." While in the twenty-first century moose have wandered back to the Adirondacks and have slowly reestablished what appear to be sustainable populations within the blue line, the new challenge is avoiding turning the Adirondacks into a tourists' petting zoo comprising wild, and potentially dangerous, charismatic megafauna.

Later, after having moved to the Adirondacks from New York City at the age of twenty, Radford undertook an expedition to the Arctic and was reportedly murdered in Canada, having shown "very poor judgment when he tried to enforce obedience by striking an Eskimo so far from civilization," according to the *Northern Tribune* in 1915. Referred to in the article as "a young man of considerable means," Radford was apparently speared or stabbed in the back after striking an Eskimo with the handle of his whip "to enforce obedience" when the guide decided to back out of the trip farther north into the Canadian wilds. Radford is said to have died on June 5, 1912, just a couple of years after having moved from New York City to North Creek.

In what appears to be a case of historical embellishment and overdramatization, nearly a half century after his death, Radford's demise was more graphically and perhaps more sympathetically—at least toward Radford, if not toward Canada's indigenous communities—rendered. This description appeared in the *Tupper Lake Free Press* in 1960: "He was pounced upon by those in whom he had placed his confidence—his Eskimo guides—murdered in cold blood and left to rot somewhere along a frozen Arctic trail or to be devoured by the wild beasts for which he had given his whole life," a rather romanticized departure from descriptions of Radford's demise around the time of his death. Whether Radford's death was murder or self-defense will likely never be known with any certainty. Nevertheless, several newspaper accounts from that period suggest that Radford initiated the confrontation, physically provoking an indigenous Canadian guide.

In another apparent whitewashing of history, at least when juxtaposed against often contradictory newspaper reports about his life as it was unfolding, Radford was lauded decades after his death in the *Adirondack Daily Enterprise* as "a noted authority on the Adirondacks," claiming that "his influence on Adirondack affairs has never been equaled" and further asserting that he was killed "by the spears of Eskimo guides over some apparent misunderstanding caused by the language barrier"—another confounding canonization of an Adirondack icon, given available reportage of Radford's life and death. Yet the privileged and inexperienced Radford, like the prodigal and mercurial Murray before him, came to represent a personification of an early Adirondack culture of pseudo-self-reliance and adventurism, leaving a persistent legacy of misinformed protectionism and lack of regard for the health and sustainability of local communities, ecosystems and economies.

2
SUSPECT SCRIBBLINGS

I fear that the exaggerations will continue to fuel the conflicts surrounding the Park and the Forest Preserve.
—*McMartin,* The Great Forest of the Adirondacks

Not unlike the confounding treatment of its putative heroes and icons by Adirondack historians, the early written history of the Adirondack experience can at times come across as a messy mélange of misinformation and obfuscation, interrupted by an occasional accuracy. It's a sort of inbred, running chronicle—too often uncited and unsubstantiated—informed and sometimes written by, and too often about, wealthy downstate lawyers, clergymen, bankers and backwoods dilettantes. These were men with names like Headley, Hammond, Colvin, and Longstreth, whose interests in the local Adirondack experience and culture appeared to be somewhat limited. More careful historians like McMartin have made valiant attempts at trying to recalibrate and demystify Adirondack history based on information found in state reports and other public documents. For our purposes, however, it is perhaps most relevant to begin with the history of the Adirondacks as suggested by the state entity charged with the Park's land-use planning and implementation.

An Adirondack Mythology

McMartin, a careful chronicler of the Adirondack experience, suggested that hyperbole and a lack of respect for and attention to the existing data have resulted in misinformed advocacy among many Adirondack historians. A notable example is the APA's contorted take on Adirondack history. According to its online Citizen's Guide to the Adirondack Park Agency Land Use Regulations, the APA was created in 1971 as an agency in New York State government "to develop long-range land use plans for public and private lands within the boundary of the Park.…The Agency strives to conserve the Park's natural resources and assure that development is well-planned" through the APA's administration of various acts.

Yet, the APA provides only limited and sometimes misleading justification for the creation of an Adirondack Park for which it is the managing authority. Adding to a growing litany of disconnects about the Park, the APA highlights the "destruction of Adirondack forests…a growing concern after 1850," a time during which, at least until the latter part of the century, spruce and other softwood species were selectively harvested proximate to water bodies for transportation downstream, as we've discussed briefly and will elucidate further. Suggesting that in the Adirondacks after the Revolutionary War "lumbermen were welcomed to the interior with few restraints," the APA relies on quotes from several early Adirondack wanderers, beginning with the tottering downstate clergyman turned historian, Joel T. Headley, to support its thesis of the "destruction of Adirondack forests."

But Headley doesn't mention forest destruction in his 1849 account, *The Adirondack: or Life in the Woods*, the work upon which the APA relies. Indeed, it is unclear how much of Headley's book describes events that actually occurred in the Adirondacks, so ambiguous were both his writing and his reputation as a reliable historian, even among some of his contemporaries. In addition, Headley appeared to apply a rather sweeping geographical definition to what he considered the Adirondacks. For example, for some of its assertions about the region, *The Adirondack* references a "vast plateau to Albany," not the mountains of the Adirondack region, which no one at the time nor since would likely mistake for a plateau. It's also unclear, and impossible to discern from his writing, whether the plateau to which he refers extends north to Albany or south from the edge of the Adirondacks. In addition, Headley claims that the region that he describes as the Adirondacks is "about the size of Massachusetts and Connecticut put together"—an area of more than 8.5 million acres, 2.3 million acres larger than even the current and still expanding Adirondack Park. Indeed, the Adirondack forest preserve in 1901, a half century after *The Adirondack* was published, comprised only 1,325,851 acres with a total Park acreage of 3,226,144 acres, according to the 1902 Seventh Annual Report of the Forest, Fish and Game Commission. It does seem clear that, when writing about the Adirondack region—what he referred to as "the central portion of New York, in which the scenes of this work are laid, and through which I traveled"—Headley was describing a place that extended far beyond what we would think of as being the Adirondacks. Indeed, while Headley is sometimes specific as to the town from which he was writing, at other times, he was quite vague, describing the general setting of his journey and his writings variously as "the wilderness of central New York" and the "Plateau of Northern New York," the latter of which may have referred to the then heavily timbered Tug Hill Plateau, located to the southwest of what is generally considered the Adirondack region.

To further muddle the matter, Headley also positioned some of his Adirondack narrative in the "backwoods." However, Headley's sense of the term *backwoods* is a bit confounding, with entire sections of his 1850 *Letters from the Backwoods and the Adirondac* describing his experiences in the forests of the south shore of Long Island. Further clouding the authenticity of his backwoods experiences, Headley himself admits in the preface of *The Adirondack: or Life in the Woods* that "The Moose Lakes described in one of the letters, I have never seen, but a friend of mine, who has once been through the wilderness with me, furnished the material, and for the sake of uniformity, I used it as my own." Headley never mentions the name of his "friend."

What Headley does describe is a region of "unbroken wilderness, crossed by no road, enlivened by no cultivation." Observing from a side hill opposite a wooded area on the edge of a black "foller" (a local distortion of the word *fallow* field, which was black most likely because it had been recently cut and burned, consistent with the farming culture of the period), he then describes with some sense of wonder and admiration the practice of "driving trees," what would be referred to today as domino felling. And, in inspirational terms, he describes his own felling of a tree for the first time, beginning the narrative with the question: "Did you ever fell a tree? If not, the experiment is worth your while—for the consciousness of power it awakens, and the absolute terror it inspires, as the noble and towering fabric at length yields to your assaults, amply repay your labor." Headley did not appear to be opposed to cutting trees or to logging—in the Adirondacks or anywhere

This page: Where was Headley during his mid-nineteenth century ramble through the Adirondacks, and what did he witness? Lake Henderson (*top*) and Raquette Lake. *Both from Headley's 1849* The Adirondack; or Life in the Woods.

else—and, indeed, seemed genuinely intrigued and personally invigorated by it. When quoting Headley to provide a rationale for its existence, none of these passages appear in the APA's selective version of Adirondack history.

Headley's 1849 work also describes a bushwhack to the peak of Mount Tahawus, today's Mount Marcy, at 5,344 feet the highest peak in the Adirondacks. Looking in all directions from the summit, Headley described "one vast wilderness seamed here and there by a river whose surface you could not see, but whose course you could follow by the black winding gap through the tops of the trees....Through out [*sic*] the wide extent but three clearings were visible—all was as Nature made it." If the few clearings that Headley could make out were man-caused, history again suggests that he was likely viewing openings that had been cleared of trees and then burned by farmers preparing forestland for conversion to agriculture.

Yet, in its "History of the Adirondack Park," the APA appears to selectively quote from Headley's *The Adirondack* to provide a narrative that appears to support the agency's origins. According to the APA, Headley wrote: "You have no conception of the quantity of lumber that is taken every winter....A great deal of land is bought of government solely for the pine on it, and after that is cut down, it is allowed to revert back to the State to pay its taxes." Here is what Headley actually wrote, apparently scribbling from Schroon Lake during the month of August:

> *After the description I have given of the wilderness and its extent, I seem to hear you inquiring, "What do people live on there?" Well, not much of anything, yet money is made in this region—that is, out nearer the settlements. You have no conception of the quantity of lumber that is taken every winter from some part of this vast plateau to Albany. A thousand people will be in the woods, where, in the summer, there is not a living being. Speculators buy the land for the sake of the timber, and then in the winter carry in provisions, etc., for the lumbermen who are to cut it...a great deal of land is bought of government solely for the pine on it; and after that is cut down, it is allowed to revert back to the state to pay its taxes. In the more central regions, however, there is no timber cut, as it is impossible to get it to market; but as civilization extends, the interior of the Empire State will, no doubt, be reached by roads, or water navigation.*

When mentioning the ambiguously placed "more central regions," it may be reasonable to assume that Headley was referencing the more remote Adirondack region, rather than the broader area of New York north of

Albany, but even that is not completely certain. "The settlements" that Headley places in this region of a "vast plateau to Albany" do not appear to describe the Adirondack mountain region, the APA's interpretation notwithstanding.

In addition, Headley's 1849 description of domino felling above a fallow clearing likely referred to an operation to create additional farmland, rather than a selective timbering operation characteristic of the period, since it appeared to have taken place in June, not during the winter logging season.[6] This was the only other reference in his 421-page book to cutting trees. Yet this is the passage that the APA edited and used to begin its history of the Adirondacks under the subheading "Exploiting the Wilderness," leading readers to believe that in 1849 the forests of the Adirondacks were being clear-cut and destroyed by loggers and therefore needed legislative protection and, later, a managing authority to enforce that mandate.

There are other aspects of Headley's narrative that don't appear to add up. For example, ordered by his physician to "go where a printed page could not meet my eye" and apparently suffering from an ambiguous, self-described "attack on the brain" (Headley appears to have suffered from a mental illness), Headley spent some time early on in Chapter IV of *The Adirondack* describing and marveling at a river drive and the skilled and dangerous work of the log drivers. Then, after observing a logjam for a while, he suddenly and impulsively joined the potentially perilous scene: "At length I threw off my coat, and laying my gun aside, also seized a 'handspike,' and was soon behind a log, tugging and lifting away." Aside from a quite reasonable skepticism about whether this actually occurred—Headley was described in Gould's 1856 *History of Delaware County* as "possessing naturally a weak constitution…unable to sustain and bear up under the labors of so vigorous and active a mind"—Headley gives us no indication of where this was all happening, or whether it was even in the Adirondacks, again describing his location only as the ambiguous "backwoods."

Beyond questions about where Headley actually was and what he was doing when writing *The Adirondack*, how reliable were Headley's Adirondack narratives? The second edition of his book received a rather positive, if not glowing, review from the *New York Times* in 1854, referring to it as "a guide" for tourists to a "vast untrodden wilderness of New York State…[that] is now within reach of every summer traveler." However, calling into question Headley's veracity, the erstwhile clergyman was described by a well-known contemporary, Edgar Allan Poe, as the "autocrat of all the quacks" and that "a book is a funny book, and nothing but a funny book, whenever it happens to be penned by Mr. Headley," reminding us of Adirondack Murray, also a sometime clergyman turned Adirondack raconteur and one of Headley's more notable contemporaries.

On its 2020 website, the APA further tethers a rationale for an Adirondack forest preserve to an Albany lawyer, abolitionist and sportsman named Samuel H. Hammond, who, in 1857, published the book *Wild Northern Scenes; or Sporting Adventures with the Rifle and Rod.* Offered in the context of APA's narrative about "destruction of Adirondack forests [that] became a growing concern after 1850," the APA extracted this single quote from Hammond: "Had I my way, I would mark out a circle of a hundred miles in diameter, and throw around it the protecting aegis of the constitution. I would make it a forest forever. It would be a misdemeanor to chop down a tree and a felony to clear an acre within its boundaries." Hammond appeared to be motivated to write this so that he could continue to exploit the region's game and to, in his words, "think, and act, and feel like a boy again."[7] Clearly, there would not only be no logging, but also no agriculture or human settlements of any kind, in Hammond's conception of the Adirondacks.

The APA selectively ignored Hammond's *Hunting Adventures in the Northern Wilds*, published a year later in 1858, which described his Adirondack sporting exploits amid "savage" and "skulking ingens" and this passage honoring a man (referred to by Hammond only as P---. C---.) who rebuilt a sawmill that was destroyed in a fire in the Adirondack town of Franklin Falls:

> *Any other man than the owner of the town, would have sunk under the calamity. Some $50,000 of his property was destroyed, and, with other embarrassments pressing upon him, the spirit of any other man would have been broken. Not so with P--- C ---. With a will that nothing could bend—an energy unconquerable as destiny—he rose up from the misfortune that overwhelmed him, defiant of fate; and scorning the power of the elements, he reared from those ashes of desolation a phoenix—stronger and better than that which destruction had swept away. Where the old mill stood, stands a better one. Hundreds of thousands of feet of lumber are piled along the road, for half a mile, and great stacks of it surround the mill. Thirty teams are drawing from these long rows of piled-up boards, and as one pile disappears, another takes its place. Where the former tavern and store stood, stands another and a better. Each dwelling-house destroyed, is replaced by a new one, and a few charred fragments, scattered about, are all that remains to remind one of the fire that made such a clean sweep of the town.*

Then switching gears to honor the notable contributions made to "civilization" by the Adirondack town's working-class lumbermen, an admiring Hammond continued:

> *Honor, I say, to all such men as P--- C---. They may be unfortunate; they may undertake more than human agency can entirely perform; they may not succeed in amassing a fortune; destiny may be against them; they may work hard and die por; they may fall; their notes may be protested;—but the world owes them a debt of gratitude. It is such men who push forward civilization—who sweep away the forests—who let the sun, with its genial influences, down upon the earth, where tall trees once obstructed his rays—who spread out green fields, and build up towns in the ancient wilderness—who give employment to labor, and impress progress upon everything around them; but they are the true "manifest destiny men"—who give to our country practical dominion over nature, by pushing civilization into the waste and desolate places in the wilderness.*

This was certainly not an endorsement for an Adirondack forest preserve, but rather an admiring approbation of rural community development and industry.

As we've seen, the APA's History of the Adirondack Park also includes references to Verplanck Colvin, who is quoted by the APA as conveying the following in his 1874 Annual Report to the Legislature: "Unless the region be preserved essentially in its present wilderness condition, the ruthless burning and destruction of the forest will slowly, year after year, creep onward—and vast areas of naked rock, arid sand and gravel will alone remain the bounty of the clouds, unable to retain it." Colvin's duplicity, or at least his confusion, is remarkable. This is the same Verplanck Colvin who was the president of a venture to build another railroad into the Adirondacks but was turned back by a judge who denied his application, admonishing Colvin, the wilderness protectionist, for his hypocrisy. And this is the Colvin who clear-cut and recklessly burned the peaks of at least two Adirondack mountains, exposing areas of naked rock where mountain ecosystems used to thrive.

Last in the APA's string of nineteenth- and early twentieth-century forest-preserve icons and advocates is T. Morris Longstreth, who had written several books, including *The Adirondacks*, published in 1917. In its 1918 book review, the *Evening Post* described Longstreth's Adirondack adventure as a "quaint mountain meander," a "story of the wanderings of two chaps, pressed neither for time nor by city obligations." The *Post* observed of the author

This page: The Benson District Three School, earliest known photo of Saranac Lake and an Adirondack hotel. Lumber from locally harvested and milled softwood logs in the nineteenth-century Adirondacks built local rural communities and summer getaways for the wealthy. School: *Hamilton County Historian*; Saranac Lake: *G.W. Baldwin*; hotel: *S.R. Stoddard photos*.

that "on the side of information on Adirondack matters, Mr. Longstreth happens to be less valuable than on the literary," criticizing him for, among other omissions, not pointing out that the worst Adirondack fire during that time "was set by a native [ed. a local Adirondacker] who refused to stop burning out his potato patch in the dry season."

The APA accurately attributes to Longstreth commentary on the state's acquisition of lands harvested by lumber interests during the Adirondacks' early pulpwood era. But Longstreth's narrative was also critical of tourists and sportsmen, especially for causing Adirondack wildfires. The forest "was wantonly cut and criminally devoured by fire," he wrote in *The Adirondacks*. "Forest fires annually ruined large areas; the stretches of forested country rapidly decreasing in size pointed to the complete extermination of all game" (pp. 15–16). Separating himself from those who were reluctant to implicate wealthy "sports" for the burning of Adirondack forests, Longstreth accurately cites the major causes of the fires of 1914 as smokers, railroads, fishermen and hunters, not logging and loggers as many others had. Moreover, like Headley before him, Longstreth wrote with some awe and appreciation of Adirondack logging: "In winter the whole process can be watched to the most enjoyable advantage; the falling place prepared, the sawing, and the fall, the trimming, and the cutting into logs." Longstreth's sense of working-class Adirondackers comes across as one of paternalistic admiration: "A good deal of sound thinking and real happiness exists in our natives—in fact, the center of common-sense [*sic*] lies half way between the pauper and millionaire, in the quiet nature-loving, stolid old observers of the summer people," according to Longstreth writing in the *Lake Placid News* in 1925.

Longstreth's connection to the creation of a rich man's paradise appears to be grounded in his longtime membership in the elite but controversial Lake Placid Club, a recreation and social clique founded in 1895 by Melvin Dewey and whose exclusionary practices in its early years discriminated against "Jews and other socially stigmatized groups," including African Americans. According to an early circular describing the Lake Placid Club of that period: "No one will be received as a member or guest against whom there is physical, moral, social or race objection, or who would be unwelcome to even a small minority....This invariable rule is rigidly enforced. It is found impracticable to make exceptions for Jews or others excluded, even though of unusual personal qualifications." African Americans were admitted only as servants, and people suffering or recovering from tuberculosis were also excluded. In the development of this privileged and fashionable Adirondack paradise, themes of not only wealth and influence, but also of discriminatory attitudes and practices, have emerged throughout the Park's history, as we'll see later.

The often ambiguous and contradictory works of some early Adirondack historians and more modern-day derivatives of those narratives aside, more intensive timber harvesting arrived in the Adirondacks toward the latter part of the nineteenth century, as technology developed in Germany for using wood fiber to produce paper was adopted in the United States. This resulted in a shift in logging from selectively harvested spruce to more broadly harvested softwoods to feed a burgeoning wood pulp industry. Concern over how much wood was now being harvested in the Adirondacks—from occasional spruce for lumber to more broadly harvested softwoods for paper at the end of the nineteenth century—and its visual impact on the landscape was likely understandable.

Clearly, the conversation around an Adirondack forest preserve versus a timber reserve had become muddled. But it was too late for those who at the time were opposed to a preserve. The die had already been cast in 1894, nine years after the creation of the Adirondack Park, and it came up "forever wild," Article XIV of the New York State Constitution stated: "The lands of the state, now owned or hereafter acquired, constituting the forest preserve as now fixed by law, shall be forever kept as wild forest lands. They shall not be leased, sold, or exchanged, or be taken by any corporation, public or private, nor shall the timber thereon be sold, removed or destroyed."

Inadvertently demonstrating his lack of understanding and appreciation of the attitudes of local Adirondackers, Donaldson mentioned the 1910 bond issue of $10,000,000 for the "acquisition of lands for State Park purposes" and the $7,500,000 for "the extension of the forest preserve." The proposition was approved by a majority of 150,496, with New York City carrying the referendum. However, apparently to the bewilderment of Donaldson, "not a single Adirondack county voted in favor of it." That this may have come as a surprise to Donaldson is telling, an example of just how out of touch he was with local realities and local Adirondack values and attitudes, inevitably skewing his sense of the region's history.[8]

So, who or what were Donaldson's sources for his history of a region that, for much of his time in the Adirondacks, he was only able to observe from a window in his adopted home of Saranac Lake? While McMartin relied heavily on reports of the State Forest Commission in her Adirondack histories, Donaldson observed that these reports covered "annual periods

Above: Adirondack guides and "sports," date unknown. *Paul Smith's College Joan Weill Adirondack Library Archives.*

Left: Overfishing by "sports" led Adirondack Murray to suggest that Adirondack waters be stocked by artificial means. *Paul Smith's College Joan Weill Adirondack Library Archives.*

since 1872, but were not always published annually.…In 1885 the Forest Preserve and a Forest Commission were created, and the latter began issuing reports, which have been continued by each succeeding commission up to the present time.…They were not exclusively Adirondack reports, nor do they tell more than a meager half of the story. The other half this chapter will attempt to supply." To fill in the gaps, he cites "intimate memories and valuable documents" supplied by Peter Schofield, Frank Gardner and William McConnell, "leaders in the long forest fight" who provided Donaldson "many a glimpse behind the scenes."

Unfortunately, Donaldson's exclusive sources brought only a single perspective to his narrative. For example, Schofield was an early forever-wild advocate who helped wordsmith language when the Adirondack Park

This page: Alfred Donaldson, banker turned historian, and the village of Saranac Lake during Donaldson's time. Donaldson published his two-volume *A History of the Adirondacks* in 1921. Alfred Donaldson: *from* Adirondack Daily Enterprise, *October 3, 1998*; Saranac Lake Village, circa 1920: *from an undated brochure by E.L. Gray & Co.*

was being added to the state constitution in 1894. Another supporter of an Adirondack forest preserve, Gardner, the New York Board of Trade secretary, reportedly remarked at a meeting that "the forest will never be made safe until they are put into the State Constitution." In Donaldson's rather myopic approach to Adirondack history, there appeared to be little or no effort to consult with those who might have a point of view that was different from his own.

The suspect scribblings of often out-of-touch and unreliable Adirondack historians helped to provide a context for a justification for a forever-wild Adirondacks, despite more objective and systematically gathered information that might have placed the region on a more socially and economically—even environmentally—sustainable trajectory. The vilification of a working class and local manufacturing, especially in the forestry sector, by those who chose to ignore state reports and local and statewide media reportage of the period has resulted in local service economies that are weak and one-dimensional, pivoting on seasonal and ephemeral service to tourists and second-home owners.

This is not to suggest that logging did not result in some short-term forest impacts, especially to forest aesthetics, as was observed by nineteenth-century tourists and recreationists who likely developed impressions of the Adirondack landscape from a boat and later a train car. The acceleration of logging activity in response to demand for pulp and paper at the end of the nineteenth century certainly represented a change—especially a visual one—from the earlier selective and scattered logging of large spruce and other softwoods in the Adirondacks. But despite the persistence of some careless historians and public agencies, the conflation of land clearing and subsequent burning of fallows by farmers with the aftermath of forest operations has been largely discredited, at least by the historical record of the period.

Helping to further shape an Adirondack mythology, another aspect of Adirondack history that captured the imagination of wealthy downstaters and those favoring an exclusive wilderness park was the adventurous backcountry sporting life and self-reliant and well-developed wilderness ethics in which these visitors to the Adirondacks engaged. Nothing could have been further from the truth.

"Boatloads of Jolly Campers"

As early as the mid- to late nineteenth century, it was clear that the Adirondacks had already begun to lose its grip on its connection to a reliable notion of a northeastern wilderness. The onslaught of tourists and "sports" was later referred to as "Murray's Rush." It was an assault for which Adirondack ecosystems, native fisheries and wildlife populations have paid a heavy and lasting price. The so-called sportsman of the nineteenth and early twentieth centuries was from a social class of Gilded Age elites who could afford to travel to the Adirondacks from the urban centers of the Northeast, stay at luxurious camps and hotels and hire local working-class guides and caretakers to cater to their needs. It was a hierarchical social order that would sound familiar to many longtime Adirondack residents 150 years later. The transformation of the Adirondacks from a true wilderness inhabited by a self-sufficient backcountry working class to a rich man's paradise, a park whose social, economic and environmental future would be defined by a more privileged upper class, was well underway. According to one observer of the Adirondack experience, "Early in Park history, the protection of the private Adirondacks, and its influence on the preservation of the public Adirondacks, was more a product of the Gilded Age and less the utilitarian goal of a socially conscious state….State land protection meant a tax-free wilderness for the nation's privileged class."[9]

Much of the sporting ethics and misadventures of the period appeared to be influenced by Murray's *Adventure in the Wilderness*. Indeed, Murray's book devotes an entire chapter to "Loon-shooting in a thunder-storm," describing his attempt to shoot a "confounded loon," in his words "to teach her to keep her mouth shut." Clearly, Murray and his early followers were not always held in high regard. Donaldson's description of Murray's Fools—"a Motley throng that crowded the Saratoga train bound north"—in July 1869 went like this:

> *It was obvious to the most casual observer that they were sportsmen en route for the Adirondacks. Each member was attired in the most approved style of the craft, huge felt hats, capacious boots, velveteen jackets slashed with multitudinous pockets, guns and rods of assorted sizes and patterns strapped together, knapsacks, and woolen and rubber blankets. When they conversed it was in the style of old campaigners. They talked knowingly of the "Wilderness," black flies, wild cats, and five pound* [sic] *trout; frequently consulted maps, "Murray," and the "Railroad guide." Occasionally they paused to mark the effect upon their fellow-passengers, and if they happened to catch a small boy listening with some show of attention, their faces shone with an effulgence of rapture.*

Fashionable. Self-infatuated. Utterly dependent. The early Adirondack "sports," many of whom were modeled after Murray and influenced by his writing, had arrived. However, counting oneself a member of this prestigious "motley throng" came at a price that eliminated all but the most well-to-do. Regarding the cost of sporting the Adirondack wilderness, Murray itemized the following in his book:

> *Guide-hire, $2.50 per day; board for self and guide while in the woods, $2.00 each per week; miscellanies (here is where the ten-dollar greenback come in), $25.00….Fifty dollars will pay one's travelling expenses both ways, from Boston to the Lower Saranac Lake, where you can meet your guide. From New York the expense is about the same. It is safe to say that one hundred and twenty-five dollars will pay all the expenses of a trip of a month's duration in the wilderness.*

An Adirondack guide (*left*) and his party of four. *Etching by C.R. Wallace, 1870s. Lake Placid Public Library.*

This was a sum that was out of reach of most people at that time. Upping the ante, Donaldson wrote, "Many of the guides received five dollars a day during this golden harvest" of Murray's Rush.

It should be noted that $125 in 1869 roughly translates to $2,336 150 years later; the average annual income in 1860 was $600. Radford, writing in 1905, indicated that Murray's salary while he was in his thirties as minister in Boston was as much as $20,000, "besides earning $10,000 additional annually upon the lecturne [*sic*] platform." At a rate of $2.50 to $5.00 per day for a guide, these workers were paid fairly well for the times. By comparison, average daily earnings in New England in 1870, for example, were $1.56 for nonfarm labor, $3.50 for masons and $2.97 for carpenters.[10] The monthly wage for farm labor, including board, was $19.87. An Adirondack guide who was provided board "while in the woods," as described by Murray in his accounting of expenses, would earn that monthly wage in approximately eight days, in only four days by Donaldson's estimate, although the work of the guide would have been somewhat sporadic and seasonal.

The nineteenth-century Adirondacks became an "in" place to be and, more importantly, to be seen. One of Murray's Adirondack "sojourns" was described in 1873 under the title "Lake Placid and Whiteface" by T.A. Griffin, who was on an Adirondack excursion with fellow travelers. Griffin described "a delightful trip during the bright days" of July and meeting Murray, apparently by chance, at the Point of Rocks railroad station in the Adirondacks. "Here we found 'Adirondack' Murray and party of nearly forty ladies and gentlemen, including Dr. Eben Tourjee,[11] attired in every variety of costume, in which that of the Scottish Highlanders and the Tyrolese seemed to predominate; with boats, tackle, camp utensils, and all the paraphernalia essential to camp life for some weeks, just starting

Above: Hunting party. *Paul Smith's College Joan Weill Adirondack Library Archives.*

Middle: Stagecoach in front of Paul Smith's Hotel, circa 1890. Fashionably attired "sports" flocked to the Adirondacks following the publication of Murray's book. *Paul Smith's College Joan Weill Adirondack Library Archives.*

Bottom: Lake Placid Railway Station, 1890s. Travelers to the Adirondacks during the late nineteenth and early twentieth centuries were typically from a social class of wealthy urbanites. *Mary MacKenzie Collection, Lake Placid Library.*

on a third annual tour to the Adirondack wilds." Surely, tramping in the wilderness was not on the minds of this clique of chichi Adirondack visitors. However, ethically questionable and careless recreational practices would be imposed on the newfound wilderness by this same class of fashionably costumed Adirondack explorers, compromising some of the region's aquatic and terrestrial ecosystems.

Sporting Ethics

Murray's tall tales and their popularity among his naive, status-seeking, urban followers tacitly tangled in a contest of one-upmanship may have inadvertently given license to others to spin their own Adirondack yarns. But were the backcountry and sporting ethics of Murray and his followers out of synch with prevailing values and practices, or are we guilty of wagging our fingers at them in the rearview mirror? In the nineteenth century, there were four principal methods of hunting deer: jacking, hounding, crusting and still hunting. There were many efforts to ban deer-jacking—a practice also referred to as shooting with a jacklight, jack shooting, jack hunting and floating for deer—in New York during the mid- to late 1800s. During this period, there was considerable moral outrage about deer-jacking, much of it originating in the state's remote north country. According to the *Malone Palladium* in 1875, a few years after the publication of Murray's book: "But others, with no sense of sport, fill the waters with set lines and gill nets, steal upon the deer with the jack at night, and slaughter them at seasons when their young, left alone, must perish," suggesting that Adirondack locals may have possessed a stronger sense of hunting ethics than the region's wealthy visitor-sportsmen. Indeed, in contrast to the questionable practices of Murray and many of his followers, in 1917, the *Adirondack Record* described the fishing ethics of local Adirondackers this way: "There are several reasons why the fishing is good at Union Falls. There is a big expanse of water; there are only five rowboats, and not many know about the place except the residents of the country, who are natural conservationists. If everybody was like them there would be no use for the game protectors or the Conservation Commission, because when they get enough they quit."

Based on media reports from the period, *natural conservationist* is not a term that comes to mind when considering the brand of sportsmanship practiced by Murray and his followers. According to one estimate reported in *On the*

Saint Lawrence and Clayton Independent in 1892, "more than half of the deer wounded by shots behind a jack light escape into the woods and die where their carcasses are never found." The would-be wildlife conservationist Radford defended and idolized the man who not only helped to popularize deer-jacking in the Adirondacks but also bragged about inventing better ways of practicing this assault on the region's deer herd. The same year, the popular weekly journal *Forest and Stream* weighed in on Murray's sense of sportsmanship: "One impression remains. In his chapter, 'When to Visit the Adirondacks,' Mr. Murray says: 'July is the best month for jack and night shooting,' I have been over the ground of night shooting, and have no more to say of it, but I would like to have Dodge or some other game protector catch him shooting deer in July."[12] Indeed, Murray dedicates a section of chapter 1, titled "The Wilderness," to "Ladies' outfit" and an entire chapter to "Jack-shooting in a Foggy Night." The book's first illustration depicts someone jacking deer while wearing a headlamp designed by Murray for that purpose—hunting deer at night by torchlight that freezes deer, making them easier to shoot. According to Murray, jack-shooting is "the most exciting of all sport—deer-shooting at night," going on to describe a dubious occurrence in which a deer that was grazed by a bullet from Murray got up and ran about with Murray's guide hanging onto its tail only to be eventually drowned by the guide as Murray slit its throat. While such an encounter would raise eyebrows among Adirondack locals, urbanites unfamiliar with the backcountry were likely much more naive.

Even Adirondack guides were overwhelmingly opposed to deer jacking, also called "floating," according to a survey of Adirondack hotel proprietors and guides conducted by the *Utica Herald* and reported in the *Ogdensburg Journal* in 1893. According to one guide, "We favor doing away with floating for the reason that in this kind of hunting there are five deer wounded to one killed and nine out of ten are does." Another article, this time in the *St. Lawrence Herald* in the same year, simply said that "Guides would like to have jacking done away with." Discussing amendments to state game laws in 1882 and proposing a simple law that would cover all of the "cumbersome statutes," *Forest and Stream* that year had this to say about deer-jacking: "Let spring shooting be abolished, jacking, or fire hunting, forbidden, the hunting of deer with dogs carefully restricted." A few months later, *Forest and Stream* observed: "How to stop the jacking, or fire-hunting of deer in the Adirondacks is a different problem and one which may claim a little of attention from our game clubs. This practice is carried on almost entirely in the close season, and is, therefore, really already forbidden, though not

Although widely considered an unethical hunting practice, Murray encouraged jacklighting. *From Alfred Billings Street's 1860* Woods and Waters, or Saranacs and Racket.

in explicit terms, as we think it should be. It is a most destructive method of hunting, and the shot that kills the old doe carries death also to two tiny spotted fawns." In 1896, *Forest and Stream* weighed in again on "dogging" and "shining" deer, this time directly implicating Murray in what was widely considered poor sportsmanship:

> *In these days, when game is steadily growing scarcer, we are becoming a trifle "finicky" as to what constitutes true sportsmanship. There was a time when "dogging" deer and "shining" deer were considered perfectly legitimate acts—the ex-reverend "Adirondack" Murray approved of them, anyhow—but hyperfinical* [sic] *sportsmen have of late condemned such methods because they do not give the game a fair chance for their lives. It may also be said that they give the pot-hunters a better chance than the highly moral sportsman has. The latter knows when he has killed enough and quits; the former keeps on killing as long as there is anything to kill, and then brags about his big score.*

Local north country newspapers also criticized these practices. In the *Ogdensburg Journal* in 1890, for example, hounding was described as "more sportsmanlike" than creeping up to a deer in a canoe with a jacklight. "The latter seems to require no more skill, other than that of the quiet movement of the guide who propels the canoe, than it does to shoot a pet lamb in a

The exclusive Saranac Lake House, seen here in 1865, attracted wealthy "sports" to the Adirondack wilderness. *S.R. Stoddard, the New York Public Library.*

farmer's dooryard." Yet even hounding was illegal in Maine and other New England states, as well as many midwestern and western states, by the late nineteenth century.

By 1896, deer-jacking was already illegal in several states, including Maine, South Carolina, Florida, Tennessee, Michigan, Minnesota, Wisconsin and Oregon. There was increased scrutiny of New York's deer-jacking situation in the mid-1890s as legislation was considered to ban the practice both on moral grounds and out of concern about declining deer herds. In 1896, deer-jacking in New York was limited by law to the period from September 1 through September 15. The practice, along with hounding, was restricted for a period of five years beginning in 1897. An amendment to the state game laws shortened the time for jacking by seventeen days, limiting the practice to nine days. According to an account critical of the practice, printed in Potsdam's *Commercial Advisor* in 1893, "Those who hunt deer with jacks, and who allow so many to go away in the woods and die, would have only nine days for that sport." By the early 1900s, state laws prohibiting deer-jacking and other questionable deer-hunting methods had finally been codified. According to New York's 1916 *The Conservation Law in Relation*

The Hotel Ampersand, circa 1890. In its description of the hotel in 1893, the *New York Times* referred to the seasonal migration of urbanites to the Adirondacks as "the invasion of 'summerers'." *S.R. Stoddard photo, Library of Congress.*

to Fish and Game: "Wild deer may be taken only on land. No jacklighting or other artificial light, trap, saltlick, or other devices to entrap or entice deer shall be used, made or set, nor shall any deer be taken by aid or use thereof. Deer shall not be hunted, pursued or killed by any dog of either sex." Unfortunately, Murray's influence over wealthy downstate "sports" who were more than willing to follow him had likely already contributed to instability in the region's deer herd.

In the meantime, hordes of pampered, costumed "sports" from the region's urban enclaves began to carve out an Adirondack rich man's paradise. Once-pristine lakes and streams were depleted by careless overfishing by wealthy sportsmen who used unethical methods then complained about a lack of fish. Threatened and extirpated wildlife species were impacted by unethical hunting practices. Sprawling and overcrowded lakefront great camps and hotels were built. Exaggerated tales of backcountry exploits were told by fashionable and self-indulged backcountry pseudo-adventurers. This was the Adirondacks of much of the nineteenth and early twentieth centuries. So much for an Adirondack wilderness, a true conservation ethic or any credible notion of a forever-wild place.

Unfortunately, this narrative has helped to form a historical backdrop for the social, economic and political realities that would define the Adirondacks into the twenty-first century. With practices reflecting poor sportsmanship now well established—with real consequences for wildlife ecology and conservation—more direct assaults on the working class and local communities of the Adirondacks were on their way.

"INVADING ARMIES AND VAMPIRE SAWMILLS"

As we've seen, loggers of the nineteenth and early twentieth centuries were often maligned, accused by some, including downstate "adventurers" and "sports" with questionable motivations and wilderness ethics, of destroying the Adirondack forest. But state records and other firsthand accounts from the period suggested otherwise. Although timber removal by necessity temporarily alters the ecology and appearance of the forest, historic misrepresentations of the impacts of logging on the region's landscape were also common among armchair Adirondack historians, some of whom, we have seen, appeared to conflate logging with the creation of fallows by farmers and land clearing for the establishment of rural communities.

Despite having relatively little impact on mid- to late nineteenth-century Adirondack forests, especially before the advent of pulpwood harvesting, loggers were an easy target for the criticisms of those who were strict wilderness preservationists. From the perspective of occupational prestige, loggers in the northern forest were historically considered "depraved," while farmers were considered "virtuous."[13] Agriculture was considered a more reliable foundation for society than logging and lumbering. As a result, loggers were easy targets when searching for whom to blame for changes to rural landscapes, despite state reports that consistently suggested culpability among members of the farming community.

Indeed, the First Annual Report of the Forest Commission of the State of New York for the Year 1885 stated that "in no section of the Adirondack counties does lumbering take all of the forest trees." Later, in its 1892 report, the commission estimated that "the lumberman did not take more than eight trees to the acre, on an average" on the relatively few acres that were harvested each year. The Third Annual Report of the New York Fisheries, Game and Forest Commission reported in its 1897 classification of lands within the Adirondack Park that 2.5 percent of the Park (75,819 acres)

This page: Logging, Tupper Lake, and Santa Clara Lumber Company, circa 1890. The lumber industry was once the center of community life and the major economic driver in the Adirondacks. Both: *Goff-Nelson Memorial Library*.

were cleared for agriculture, while 54.2 percent (1,627,955 acres) had been selectively logged for softwood timber and 37.9 percent (1,139,593 acres) was untouched forestland. Indeed, in the previous year, the New York Fisheries, Game and Forest Commission explained that "The phrase 'lumbered land' is a somewhat misleading one. It does not imply that such land is cleared, devastated, of even stripped of timber. The term is used, locally, to describe lands from which the 'soft wood' (spruce, hemlock, pine and tamarack—one and all) has been taken, leaving the hard wood (birch, cherry, maple, beech, etc.) standing." It further asserted that there were so many trees left after "lumbering" that "an inexperienced eye glancing over it would scarcely detect the work of an axe."

Nevertheless, concern over timber harvesting was pivotal to the creation of and justification for a forever-wild forest preserve and, ultimately, the Adirondack Park. Early and more recent historians have decried the destruction of Adirondack forests, even during times when they were being harvested selectively, almost unnoticeably, according to state reports. Even

This page: Log drive in Hope and a sawmill at Hope Falls. Logs from selectively harvested softwood trees were floated to downstream mills for conversion into lumber. *Both from Hamilton County Historian.*

during the advent of more broadly applied pulpwood logging, official state records suggest that forest removal associated with commercial harvesting was grossly exaggerated.

Not unlike Colvin, Murray's view of economic development in the Adirondacks, beyond recreation, tourism and sporting, was a bit contradictory. For example, despite his heavy reliance on the forest industry to provide raw material for the paper required to publish his later writings, the influential Murray expressed a negative view of logging, stating that "lumbermen are the curse and scourge of the wilderness. Wherever their axe sounds, the pride and beauty of the forest disappear." That Murray would later be involved in a sawmill venture in Texas seems at odds with his disdain for lumbermen, a further manifestation of his rather flighty and opportunistic personality. But even Murray asserted that logging had little impact on Adirondack ecosystems. Describing logging in Maine, he wrote: "The mountains are not merely shorn of trees, but from base to summit fires, kindled by accident or malicious purpose, have swept their sides, leaving the blackened rock exposed to the eye, and here and there a few unsightly trunks leaning in all directions, from which all the branches and green foliage have been burnt away." He then erroneously asserted that "in the Adirondack Wilderness you escape this. There the lumberman has never been." Ironically, a primary cause of ecosystem impacts in the Adirondacks during this period were the droves of tourists and recreationists whom Murray was attracting to the state's north woods through his persuasive storytelling.

Again, irrespective of when logging, unconfounded by land clearing for farming and homesteading, began in the Adirondacks, one of the most common myths that has been perpetuated by some Adirondack historians is the culpability of the timber industry for rampant destruction of the Adirondack forest. The disconnect appeared to be particularly annoying to McMartin, who wrote in 1994 that "advocates of the day, writing in journals that have been preserved and are most accessible for modern study, claimed that lumbermen were responsible for most destruction. That was not the case, but modern writers have found it easier to quote these journals than to seek the truth." Unfortunately, as we shall see, this persistent trail of careless advocacy has led to the incremental development of a narrative that has been used to support a forever-wild forest preserve and, later, a National Historic Landmark, a biosphere reserve, an Adirondack Park management authority and proposals for a regionally managed Northern Forest and a federally managed Adirondack Mountains National Park. All of this had implications for the management of the Adirondack Park. Continuing,

McMartin observed: "As a result, much has been written for the centennials of the Forest Preserve and the Park claims that reaction to clearcutting was the principle cause of their establishment. No one today seems to look to the Forest Commission reports that noted that up until spruce was harvested for pulp, only the largest sawlogs were taken, that the forest was little disturbed and that such lumbering did not affect the forest's ability to retain water and release it slowly." She concluded that misinformation and exaggerations passed along as historical fact "will continue to fuel the conflicts surrounding the Park and the Forest Preserve."

As an example of what likely frustrated McMartin about some misleading and poorly cited historical threads, consider this passage, written in 1995, in stark contrast to McMartin's sense of Adirondack history based on the historical record:

> *There was a gloomy side to Adirondack logging. By 1898, after more than thirty years of hard cutting, nearly two-thirds of the region's forest had been logged for softwoods. In retrospect, it was a litany of disaster. Virgin forest stands were completely lumbered.…Devastation by loggers prompted action. Between 1885, when the Forest Preserve was created, and 1894 the state experimented with statutory protection. Finally, the Constitutional Convention of 1894 ratified what is known as the forever wild clause, Article VII, which became constitutional law in New York in January 1895.*[14]

There appears to be little, if anything, in the historical record that supports these assertions for the period 1868–98—the author's frame of reference—yet they persisted, comprising a significant chapter of an anti-logging Adirondack mythology. For example, compare this historian's perspective with this passage from the state's first State Forest Commission report, published 110 years earlier in 1885: "An experienced person viewing a piece of Adirondack land would be unable to tell from its general appearance or from a glance over the tops of trees whether it has been lumbered or not," it stated. The Adirondack region "with but little exception is but unbroken wilderness." Nearly a century later, those statements from the first Forest Commission Report were expanded on by McMartin.: "Many reasons explain why logging before 1890 did so little to alter the Adirondack forest landscape" (p. 38), she wrote in 1994. Before 1890, "nothing in the heart of the Adirondacks had been clear cut; in fact, most tracts had not been cut at all. Because only spruce, hemlock, and pine were logged, as late as 1885 no more than fifteen to thirty percent of the forest cover had been taken from little more than a third of the original park."

During this period, spruce was cut selectively based on its size and its proximity to water, river drives being the only reliable form of transportation for spruce logs from logging sites to downstream mills where they were converted to lumber. It was not until the early 1890s that the development of the railroad allowed cutting over much larger areas, alleviating the restriction of harvesting of trees based on their proximity to water. Speaking of the ephemeral visual effects of harvesting at the turn of the century in the Adirondacks, Superintendent of Forests for the State of New York Colonel William Fox, writing in the 1898 Third Annual Report of the Commissioners of Fisheries, Game and Forests, alluded to the proportion of spruce cut on what he referred to as "lumbered lands"—"tracts from which the spruce and, perhaps, some other conifers, have been removed"—as "being so small that its removal makes little change in the appearance of the forest or decrease in the mass of foliage. After three or four years, when the tops and limbs left by the lumbermen have been crushed to the ground by successive snowfalls and rotted there, and the underbrush has concealed the stumps, persons unacquainted with the composition of these forests would not notice any trace of the log chopper's work."

A few years later, in 1902, in an attempt to further clarify the distinction between lumbering and clearing for farming, Fox wrote the following in a seminal report titled "History of the Lumber Industry in the State of New York" for the New York State Sixth Annual Report of the Forest, Fish, and Game Commission:

> *Right here attention is called to the fact that from the days of the first settlement down to the present time the lumbermen have never resorted to clearing operations in carrying on their work of tree felling. There is, however, a widespread impression to the contrary. People are very apt to think of cleared lands and farming areas as the result of lumbering operations, and to attribute the absence of forests to the work of the lumbermen.*

Fox continued to shed light on the impacts associated with agricultural practices compared with those associated with timber removal during the late nineteenth century: "The farmer cuts and burns every tree and bush to make his clearing and improve his land; the lumberman takes only a few scattered trees in the acre, confining his selection to some merchantable species….Had no one ever landed on our shores but lumbermen, had no

other industry but theirs ever been carried on within our borders, the forests of our State would still be standing in an unbroken, umbrageous growth." Despite these on-the-ground observations by the State Forest Commission and later the Commission of Fisheries, Game and Forests, historians and other observers of the Adirondack landscape continued to implicate logging, and therefore much of the region's working class, for many of the Park's landscape-scale afflictions.

State Forest Commission reports from the late nineteenth and early twentieth centuries notwithstanding, Donaldson offered this rather contradictory narrative:

> *The march of the lumberman was like that of an invading army—they attacked and destroyed the outposts first, and only gradually made their way to the inner citadel. They did damage, because they lumbered carelessly, with no concern for the future. Their worst sin was the fire menace that they left behind, and which caused incalculable destruction. Their damage to the superficial appearance of the woods, however, was negligible. Only the largest conifers were felled in the early days. All other trees were left standing. As a consequence, the spring foliage would often camouflage the traces of a winter's cut.*

Donaldson's insistence on misinformation and hyperbole is just one example of the divisive exaggerations to which McMartin would refer some decades later and that helped support future efforts to create a rich man's paradise at the expense of local Adirondack communities and their economies. Referring to lumbermen, Donaldson continued his rant, asserting that "their sins were many," with their "vampire sawmills at Glens Falls, Sandy Hill, and Fort Edward." Donaldson and many Adirondack wanderers and historians who pre-dated and succeeded him were not finished blaming the logging industry for the perceived afflictions of the Adirondacks. Loggers were also indicted for events far more damaging than the felling of scattered spruce or the subsequent harvesting of softwoods for pulp, propping up a justification for an elitist notion of a forever-wild forest preserve and the misleading rhetoric that supported it.

This page and opposite: Early homesteading and community establishment in the Adirondacks: Bloomingdale (*opposite*), Blue Mountain (*top*) and Indian Lake (*bottom*). Inexperienced nineteenth-century observers of the Adirondack landscape appeared to mistake land clearing for clear-cutting by loggers. Bloomingdale: *S.R. Stoddard photos*; Blue Mountain: *Library of Congress*; Indian Lake: *Hamilton County Historian*.

"THE LUMBERMEN CAUSE NO FIRES"

As we alluded to earlier, running parallel to the often distorted and exaggerated criticisms of logging and the continued marginalization of the region's working-class logging community, there is substantial, and perhaps intentional, mythology related to the lumber industry's culpability for Adirondack wildfires, especially the severe fires of the late nineteenth and early twentieth centuries. Unraveling this mythology provides a sense of the degree to which Adirondack history has often been carelessly and chronically storified, provides an understanding of the motivations of those who were critical of the logging industry and offers additional context for the subsequent evolution of the Adirondacks as a rich man's paradise of declining year-round populations and inflexible local economies.

McMartin's carefully researched writing has not dissuaded historians from fabricating and then passing along as fact their own version of the lumber industry's culpability for wildfires, perpetuating a myth that appeared to be motivated by a desire to cast the forest industry, an early driver of local Adirondack economies, in a negative light. "Throughout, advocates of the Forest preserve [*sic*] have used exaggeration, hyperbole even, to win their points," she asserted in 1994. For example, although Donaldson references the eventual use of locomotives to transport logs, except for oblique references to laws that constrained the behavior of the railroads, he neglects to discuss in any detail the forest fire damage for which railways were clearly responsible.

As we've seen, while the logger of the era was a convenient scapegoat for past and more modern historians, reports of the State Forest Commission and, later, the Commissioners of Fisheries, Game and Forests and the Conservation Commission—widely available historical documents—suggest that farmers clearing the woods for agriculture and the careless behavior of recreationists were the primary causes of forest fires in the Adirondacks. Most farmer-caused fires occurred during the spring months of April and May, when they would be engaging in clearing fallows. With the advent of rail transport in the region, the negligence of railroads in not clearing their own rights-of-way and arresting sparks from their engines became more common sources of both wildfire fuel and ignition, respectively.

The severe fire risk associated with railroads eventually led to regulations that required rail companies to reduce sparks and other sources of ignition from locomotives and manage fuels along rail rights-of-way. According to the 1896 First Annual Report of the Commissioners of Fisheries, Game and Forests of the State of New York, "Every railroad company whose road passes through waste or forest lands, or lands liable to be overrun by fires within this State, shall twice in each year cut and burn off or remove from its right of way all grass, brush or inflammable material, but under proper care, and at all times when the fires thus set are not liable to spread beyond control." Other laws required the addition of spark arresters to smokestacks of locomotives and forbade the deposition of "fire coals or ashes upon their track in the immediate vicinity of woodlands."

Unfortunately, compliance by the railroads was spotty—fines were only $100 for each offense—and Adirondack wildfires became more common. In addition, the First Annual Report of the Commissioners of Fisheries, Game and Forests of the State of New York asserted that "more forest fires are traced to railroads than any other source. It is not only the operating of these roads that tends to the destruction of the State forests, but also in their construction much forest land has been stripped; in the first place, to clear off the four rods wide constituting the right of way; and in the second place many thrifty young trees have been sacrificed to supply the necessary ties, and the demand created for piling and bridge timber." The same report continues to lament the creation of railroad clearings that "mow a swath before them," thus fragmenting the forest landscape. Squatting by track construction gangs was responsible for additional forest damage proximate to railroad grades. "They start a small clearing in the woods adjacent to the railroad; fire of course is used to clear with, and, by the combined efforts of the squatters and the railroad, a belt of timber adjacent to the track is cut and burned, widening from year to year."

Adjudication over the application for an extension of a rail line into the Adirondacks filed by forever-wild advocate Verplanck Colvin occurred in 1902, years after the state had filed the reports of its Forest Commission. Colvin would have been very aware of the damage that locomotives and railroad workers could cause to the Adirondack wilderness, as well as the damage caused by the motley invasion of Murray's Fools and Radford's "thronged carries and trails," impacts that Colvin's railway would have only exacerbated. Equally curious, and supporting McMartin's assertion of hyperbole and the vilification of the forestry sector by modern-day historians, more definitive, documented counter-observations are ubiquitous in the historical record. One of the earliest such documents is the First Annual Report of the Forest Commission of the State of New York, which described at length the causes of wildfires and the resulting damage farmers were bringing to the region's soil fertility:

> *From the reports of our own special agents, we find that forest fires originate from the following named causes: From burning over recently chopped sections or fallow, with a view of clearing the land for agricultural purposes, where the timber is merely felled and lies in a tangled mass. The chopping is usually done in the winter and the "fallow" burned in the spring and the coming out of the leaves when everything is as dry as tinder. The farmer or settler selects this time because he is then more sure of making a complete clearing. Regard is seldom paid to the direction of force of the wind, and, ordinarily, when once started, the fire is allowed to take care of itself. In this manner it gets headway, and, reaching the adjoining forest, spreads rapidly, and soon gets beyond control.... Farmers find that after about three years cutting on these meadows, the grass gets matted down, and they then burn them over. These fires spread to the woods, causing large tracts of timber to be destroyed. This is repeated every few years until the soil on the neighboring mountains is entirely burned off. There are many such places along the Saranac river, in Essex county.*

It's important to reiterate that farmers were not loggers. However, farmers of the period were, of necessity, amateur woodcutters who cleared their own land and burned felled trees and brush to prepare their land for planting. According to Fox, writing in the 1902 Sixth Annual Report of the Forest, Fish and Game Commission: "Many of the fires which destroyed so much of our forest areas were due largely to the carelessness of the farmers in burning their brush and log heaps; also, but in a smaller degree, to locomotives, hunters, campers and several minor causes. The lumbermen do not start fires; for their work—chopping and log hauling—is done mostly in the late fall and winter when the woods will not take fire." In a real sense, across most of the rugged Adirondack landscape, encroaching forests were the enemy of agriculture and farmers were, at best, ambivalent about their existence except as a source of fuel. As reaffirmed in the Third Annual Report of the Conservation Commission, the people responsible for the severe fires of 1913 "are not woodsmen" but recreationists who "are not conversant with the conditions existing in the forest, especially as regards the danger of fire."

The State Forest Commission was not the only chronicler of the relationship between forest wildfires and fallow burning. Even the wayward historian Headley weighed in on the problems associated with clearing and burning fallows by farmers when he observed a forest fire near Schroon Lake in 1849, thirty-seven years before the first Forest Commission Report: "There has been a long drought in this section, which so dried up everything combustible, that the forest became one great tinder box, needing only a spark to make a conflagration. This was accidentally furnished by some men burning a fallow." Headley makes no mention of logging slash as a source of fuel or loggers as a source of ignition for the forest fire that he claims to have witnessed.

A few years after the State Forest Commission's first report to the legislature, the Fourth Annual Report more explicitly defended the forest products industry from spurious and inaccurate assertions about its culpability for wildfires, stating that "it will be noted with interest that the principal causes of these fires were not the ones which had hitherto been claimed as such. In no case have they been reported as originating in lumbering operations, or in the 'slash' left by log-choppers," despite claims by some latter-day historians. Consistent with previous (and subsequent) reports and the information available at the time, the Fourth Annual Report leveled blame for forest wildfires elsewhere. "The most frequent source is found in petty farming operations, and the burning of fallows; and, next, the railroads and locomotives were a prolific cause. The campers and sportsmen seem to be responsible next, while the remaining instances were due to various and, sometimes, unknown causes."

Further supporting the notion that wildfires were generally started by locomotives and careless recreationists and farmers, most fires burned not in the interior but on the edges of forests. Again, according to the State Forest Commission in 1893: "In examining the reports of the Firewardens, it will be seen that, as usual, the most prolific cause of fire was the burning of fallows or attempts at clearing land for farming purposes. For this reason, almost all the fires were on the borders of the forest, and none in the interior," further clearing loggers of culpability for creating forest-fire fuel or for wildfire ignition. But perhaps expressing the culpability for Adirondack wildfires most succinctly is this 1886 quote from a hotelkeeper from Essex County from the Forest Commission First Annual Report: "The chief trouble is from people who burn fallow to make a small clearing, and destroy the woods on two or three square miles....We don't want a man to burn over a couple of townships to clear a turnip patch."

The second most common cause of fires in the state in 1897 was abandoned campfires of sportsmen, recreationists, travelers and surveyors, reminding us of the surveying antics of Verplanck Colvin. The third was locomotives, from live coals and sparks and thrown from smokestacks, reminding us of Colvin's hypocrisy. Importantly, according to the Third Annual Report of the Commissioners of Fisheries, Game and Forests of the State of New

York, the fuel that was ignited by locomotives wasn't tree tops and branches left behind from logging—logging slash—but "dry grass, old, rotten ties, and combustible material." Some fires derived from the burning of old railroad ties, as a means to dispose of them, and from dumping ash pans from locomotives in the woods. The report went on to make the following, rather definitive statement: "The lumbermen cause no fires, despite the common impression to the contrary. During the winter, the time when they are in camp, the snow prevents forest fires."

Year after year, a reliable historical thread derived from official state reports absolved loggers and logging of any responsibility for Adirondack wildfires. The commission continued to assess the culpability for wildfires in the Adirondacks in its Fourth Annual Report, elaborating on land clearing by farmers and the burning of fallows. "The most frequent cause of woodland fires in our State are the small fires started by farmers for the purpose of burning brush, logs, and stumps, in order to clear some piece of land. These are known locally as fallow fires, and the operation is generally alluded to as burning a foller," according to the report. "It is the farmer, not the lumberman, who has destroyed so many thousands of acres of timber land. The lumberman takes only a few trees per acre of some merchantable species; the farmer in his operations destroys the entire forest," essentially reiterating both the very selective nature of logging during the period and the role of Adirondack farmers in land clearing and their carelessness with fallow fires. The same report cites other, more minor sources of ignition for wildfires, including one in the town of Fort Ann in Washington County, which was "supposed to have been started by an Italian who was shooting robins for pot pie."

New York State's various commission reports weren't the only sources of information on the causes of Adirondack wildfires. The federal Bureau of Forestry weighed in on the 1903 forest fires, while providing some insight into the subsistence and cash-crop culture of the period. "Hunters set fire to encourage the growth of grass in the spring and thus attract the deer to a known locality. Berry pickers burned land to favor the growth of berry bushes, ginseng (or "sang") gatherers to make their work more easy and profitable." The report also cited instances of wildfire ignition that had not yet been documented. For example, "in one town boys were discovered setting fire after fire for the pleasure of seeing the men hurry to fight them. In another the warden saw smoke roll up and hastening to the spot found the incendiary coolly enjoying the spectacle as the flames roared up a steep mountain side. This man had absolutely nothing to gain by his act

This page: By clearing land and carelessly burning fallow fields ("follers"), farmers were responsible for many forest fires in the Adirondacks, according to state reports. Keene Valley, circa 1990, and *Valley of the Hudson*, circa 1888. Keene Valley: *Keene Valley Public Library*; *Valley of the Hudson*: *S.R. Stoddard, Library of Congress.*

and ran some danger of losing his cabin had the wind changed." As with state reports, the Bureau of Forestry report made no mention of loggers or logging slash. The bureau, however, did clarify its description of fallow fires: "Next to the railroads, fallowing, or the clearing of land by burning debris left after lumbering, was probably the most prolific source of fire.... The law forbids such burning during the months of April and May," clearly equating the clearing of farmland with farmer-related "lumbering."

Despite logging slash being rarely implicated as a source of fuel for Adirondack wildfires, a top lopping law was enacted in the spring of 1909, requiring loggers to cut off the top and all branches of conifers at the time that the trees are cut within forest preserve counties. While top lopping was a reasonable approach to reducing ground fuels, if it had any value at all the practice likely served only to cool down some forest fires that had already been started in a fallow or railroad right-of-way, or by a recreationist's campfire or fisherman's smoking. It did not address the primary sources of ignition and fuels for those fires. It remained, however, that, while new regulations were being promulgated to control the clearly destructive practices related to farming and railroads, far less was done to regulate the careless behaviors of Adirondack "sports" and other tourists and recreationists.

In 1911, New York State established the Conservation Commission, which took on the powers and duties of the Forest, Fish and Game Commission, the Forest Purchasing Board and the Water Supply Commission. Even under the new Conservation Commission, however, the reported causes of Adirondack wildfires were consistent with what had been reported by the earlier Forest Commission and, later, the Forest, Fish and Game Commission, with the exception that lightning fires appeared to have become more prevalent. This helped dispel any notion that these two earlier commissions were favoring the forestry sector in their reports of wildfire culpability. According to data gathered by the Conservation Commission, the primary causes of Adirondack fires of 1911 were familiar: railroads (67), lightning (65), smokers (60), fishermen (32), berry pickers (32), clearing land (31), incendiary (30), carelessness (30), campers (27) and hunters (9).[15]

Significantly, speaking against a forever-wild forest preserve and in favor of multiple-use forest management, subsequent Conservation Commission reports advocated for the utilization of trees on the forest preserve—essentially treating it more as a timber reserve—in part to reduce the natural accumulation of woody fuels through wind throw and decay. According to the Second Annual Report of the Conservation Commission, transmitted to the state legislature on January 5, 1913: "The leaving of trees to decay not only destroys the beauty of the forest and hampers its growth, but is also an actual menace to safety....That the intent of the framers of the Constitution, when they prohibited the removal, sale or destruction of timber within the forest preserve, can have been to prevent the removal of dead and down timber, is hard to believe....In all logic, the fundamental law should be amended so as to permit the removal of dead timber," thereby reducing the natural accumulation of potentially hazardous forest fuels.

Nevertheless, Donaldson and many Adirondack historians, storytellers and forever-wild advocates since his time have continued to insist on vilifying the logging industry for this "ruthless and reckless warfare on the forests" by laying blame for Adirondack wildfires on loggers, despite overwhelming evidence in the historical record that would suggest otherwise. If there was any "warfare" on the forests of the Adirondacks, it was brought by careless farmers, recreationists and railroad companies, not loggers as suggested by both Donaldson in his poorly informed rant against the lumber industry and by modern-day historians and others who picked up and ran with this deceptive thread. When researching his *History of the Adirondacks* leading up to its publication in 1921, Donaldson had access to the reports cited here and referenced them in his narrative. But even if he could not get his hands on the annual reports of the state commissions, at a minimum Donaldson would have had direct access to local newspapers, whose reportage on Adirondack wildfires were in general agreement with, and in many cases derived from, official state reports.

For example, midway through Donaldson's ten-year effort to write his book, the *New York Times* reported that the large Adirondack fires of 1915 were attributed to a fisherman who dropped a match into "tinderlike undergrowth." A month later, the *Times* quoted the state's conservation commissioner as saying that "nearly all the forest fires are caused by

Forest fire in the Adirondack High Peaks, 1913. As outdoor recreation, the accumulation of woody fuels and climate change collide, conditions for severe Adirondack wildfires will become more prevalent. *Keene Valley Public Library Archive.*

carelessness … The principle trouble is in leaving the campfire." None of this was mentioned by Donaldson, who chose instead to implicate an easier target: the Adirondack timber industry and its "invading army" of working-class woods workers and "vampire sawmills." He was perhaps motivated, in part, by a desire to run interference for his wealthy friends and other privileged Adirondack tourists and sportsmen of the period and to severely limit logging in the Adirondacks in favor of a more gentrified "people's playground"—an outcome for which the stage was now set.

PART II

FOREVER-WILD PARK POLITICS

We want no landed aristocracy in these mountain wilds, to hold and use to the exclusive enjoyment of themselves and their money-titled kind great private preserves, as in the monarchies of the old world, whereon the sovereign people of the state may not trespass and where the laws designed to protect wild life of the forest may be set at naught.
—Lake Placid News, *1915*

In many respects, wealthy Americans bought the Adirondacks for wealthy Americans.
—Erickson, "In Search of Sustainable Development"

3
RICH MAN'S PARADISE

The Adirondack park scheme seems to me one of the most stupendous humbugs which ever received the attention and support of intelligent man.
—Thompson in the Plattsburgh Sentinel, *1884*

Established by the New York State legislature in 1885, the now six-million-acre Adirondack Park is 87 percent forested. The Park covers an area approximately the size of the state of Vermont and includes parts or all of New York's twelve northern counties and 103 municipalities with approximately 128,000 residents. It has doubled in size since its creation and currently represents one-fifth of the state's land area. With the adoption of Article XIV, Section 1 of the New York State Constitution in 1894, the Adirondack Forest Preserve was created, with a forever-wild constitutional mandate within preserve lands. Almost half of the lands within the Adirondack Park are designated preserve, a proportion that is growing as the state acquires additional lands to add to the Park. It is the country's largest National Historic Landmark.

While preservationists of the era expressed apprehension about the environmental impacts of timber harvesting in the Adirondacks, influential New York City merchants and industrialists were ostensibly more concerned that timber harvesting would reduce water flows to the Hudson River and Erie Canal. Given that history, in the form of state reports and newspaper accounts, tells us that timber harvesting at the time of the creation of the Park was limited to occasional trees located near waterways and that logging's impacts to downstate water flows were quite speculative, it seems likely that the creation of a preserve may have been driven by other interests and rationales, including providing a buffer between wealthy Adirondack "sports" and local, working-class residents. This notion is supported, for example, by a failed attempt to designate a federally managed national park in the Adirondacks, with lines drawn to exclude the estates of some wealthy and influential Adirondack estate owners. The failure ultimately led to the creation of a managing authority empowered to control growth in the Park; an aborted bid to create a regionally regulated northern forest that looked to the Adirondack Park experiment as a model; and the foisting of an Adirondack biosphere reserve designation on an unsuspecting Adirondack public.

ROCKY RELATIONSHIPS

In her 1992 paper describing a rich man's paradise, Louise Halper observed that, in the "constitutionalization" of the Adirondack Park, "forest resources were withdrawn from the market by popular demand and thereby saved."[16] However, the motivation behind a forever-wild forest preserve was not merely preservationist or altruistic, but rather related to enhancing "the recreational value of the great Adirondack estates of wealthy downstaters, a cross-section of the social and financial elites of New York and of the country." Murray's followers and their descendants, seeking an exclusive Adirondack resort, were beginning to form an alliance to save the Adirondacks from those who did not share their values and social class, except for the few locals who were needed to provide services to estate owners. Halper asserted further: "The Forest Preserve provided Adirondack estate owners with an impenetrable barrier of public lands maintained at public expense, and on which the state paid taxes....To this day local residents resent state involvement and the Park's very existence." Halper's assertions echoed those of Adirondack region sawmill owner Lemon Thompson,[17] who over one hundred years earlier observed that "men who have leisure and money, position and influence...imagine that if the State owned a great wilderness park that they could claim as a common inheritance and enjoy without restraint that they could find in such a retreat, away from the pomp and show of busy life, quiet and happiness in fishing and hunting such as they could not enjoy elsewhere. All this class of persons are active and vociferous in demanding the establishment of an Adirondack park." Conservation, as we have seen with Murray's followers, did not appear to be a primary motivation among this group, if it registered at all. On the contrary, the overriding ethic of the time seemed more centered on resource exploitation—"sporting"—and a carefree and careless disregard for the integrity and sustainability of ecosystems, both natural and human.

Early environmental groups were populated by wealthy downstaters and large Adirondack landowners, motivated to form a buffer between their estates and the working-class Adirondack public. Similar to the motivations of Adirondack Murray, their environmental agenda was dominated by a sense of preserving their own interests, rather than in preserving the ecological integrity of the Park or finding a sustainable synergy between ecology and community. This is neither a new interpretation nor the isolated point of view of writers who, like Halper and others, came later. In 1906, the *Adirondack News* ran a story titled "Millionaires Object," describing the Association for the Preservation of the Adirondacks as "a corporation which has named among its trustees J. Pierpont Morgan, William G. Rockefeller, Alfred G. Vanderbilt and Harry Payne Whitney and is composed almost entirely of millionaire park owners." Continuing, the report commented on the differences between wealthy Adirondack "sports" and tourists and local, working-class Adirondackers:

> *Their idea of the uses to which the Adirondack region should be put differs widely from that of the people who live in the Adirondacks and bordering country. The millionaire conception of the proper manner of preservation and use of this great area is to own and enclose with wire fences vast tracts for the enjoyment of the owner and his guests, employing great numbers of watchmen and wardens to warn off the public and drive people away, and retaining lawyers to prosecute trespassers.... The development of the resources of the state is of no concern to them, unless it adds to their accumulations.*

Some years later, while discussing the 1902 formation of the Association for the Protection of the Adirondacks, Donaldson rather defensively presented a counterargument. Stating that "others sought to belittle it as a combination of rich men and large landowners who were primarily seeking advantages for themselves and their preserves," he went on to say that "this impression still obtains to some extent, but nothing could be further from the truth," followed by the rather oblique assertion that "the members of the association have reaped such personal benefits from it only as must accrue to the individual from any improvement of general conditions." Contradicting Donaldson's contentions, some two decades earlier, in 1902, the *New York Times* referenced the association with the headline "To preserve Adirondacks: Wealthy owners of estates in the mountains form an association for this purpose." The article described the membership as "owners of large private estates, parks, and preserves in the Adirondack region," with an office in New York City.

Donaldson's comments about the forever-wild motivations of wealthy Adirondack landowners were likely further biased by his background as the offspring of a banking family from New York City and that his inner circle in Saranac Lake comprised many of the local elites of the day, including John Black (an Andover Academy and Princeton graduate whose family owned the Ohio Brass Company) and William Minshull (a New York City banker and cofounder with Donaldson of the Adirondack National Bank). What does seem clear is that he chose to ignore primary sources of documented information when writing about the creation of the Park and the region's forests, forest fires and forest politics. This despite claims that, while writing *A History of the Adirondacks*, he described himself as "quite concerned with veracity," using "every possible avenue of material collection at his disposal" and that he "assembled a private research library which soon contained all of the printed material pertaining to the region that he could lay his hands on," according to the *Adirondack Daily Enterprise* in 1987.

It is perhaps a bit disingenuous, although, given his background, not too surprising, for Donaldson to have omitted that among the association's first elected officers—all of whom, if one believes Donaldson, looked out for the interests of the masses rather than simply their narrow self-interests—were the following: William G. Rockefeller (son of Standard Oil cofounder William A. Rockefeller Jr., owner of the sprawling Bay Pond preserve located in the northern Adirondacks); Warren Higley (a judge who was president of the Adirondack League Club, a private and exclusive organization and large Adirondack landowner that was founded in the 1890s, around the time that an Adirondack preserve was created); James McNaughton (first president of the McIntyre Iron Work, who ascended Mount Marcy with Theodore Roosevelt and four others on September 13, 1901, when Roosevelt heard the news that President McKinley's condition had worsened after being shot in an assassination attempt in Buffalo); William C. Whitney (former secretary of the navy who also had a string of banking and corporate interests, including the exploitation of coal and iron resources in eastern Canada); and Edwin S. Marston (secretary of the Farmers' Loan and Trust Company). Whitney was one of the largest landowners in the eastern United States and had close family connections to the Rockefellers, who had had run-ins with local Adirondackers over the family's inability or unwillingness to coexist with working-class neighbors and communities in the Park. Henry Harper, from the Harper publishing family in New York City, was a secretary of the Association for the Protection of the Adirondacks and is said to have been committed to stopping logging in the Adirondacks, despite his publishing business's heavy reliance on paper for its very existence. Whatever may be said of the individuals comprising this group, it was not an assemblage devoid of "leisure and money, position and influence" nor without a clear vested interest in the disposition of the Park, generally for their own enjoyment and to the exclusion of others, a recurring theme in Adirondack history.

The thread of historical misinformation and ambiguity related to the creation of a rich man's paradise in the Adirondacks continued to stubbornly persist, some latter-day historians accepting the poorly documented assertions of Donaldson and others. For example, defending the influential Adirondack League Club and naively deferring to Donaldson as having presented an objective point of view, in 1955, P.F. "Fay" Loope, founder of the Schenectady Chapter of the Adirondack Mountain Club, stated in the *Adirondack Daily Enterprise* that "the Adirondack League Club has been pictured as a small group of corpulent gentlemen with money sticking out of each of their pockets who are greedily hanging onto a section of land in the Adirondacks and keeping you and me out of land that is rightfully ours.... Let's look at the facts by referring to *A History of the Adirondacks* compiled by Alfred L. Donaldson and published in 1921," suggesting that Donaldson must have had it right. Loope went on to describe the Adirondack League Club and the reasons for its formation: "The League was formed in 1890 by a small group of wealthy men who were dedicated to preserving the wild aspects of the Adirondack forests. At this time lumbermen were mowing down thousands of acres of forests with complete disregard for fire prevention, future needs, or the rights of the State of New York. State lands were plundered of their trees." In addition to scrambling his facts about the Adirondack logging industry's well-documented lack of culpability for forest clearing and wildfires in the late 1880s and 1890s, Loope would likely be surprised to see the Adirondacks today, where, on well-managed private lands, the forests are healthier and less prone to fire than those on many neighboring forest preserve lands.

Tensions between Adirondack residents and wealthy Adirondack landowners from downstate appeared to have sometimes devastating implications for the region. Writing in 1903, H.M. Suter, an agent of the USDA Bureau of Forestry, asserted that "the rapid increase in the number and extent of private parks and game preserves in the Adirondacks, and the resulting decrease in the area open to all for hunting and fishing, have engendered strong feeling against private preserves upon the part of some who do not enjoy their privileges....The strong feeling in parts of the Adirondacks against private preserves is therefore an exceedingly serious menace of continued damage from fire." Describing the devastating fires of 1903, even Donaldson had to agree that there were tensions between local residents and more privileged outsiders that may have resulted in retribution in the form of arson against wealthy Adirondack landowners, observing that "the largest fire of all...was on the Rockefeller Preserve, where 40,000 acres were devastated."

Whether the severe fires of 1903 that had a catastrophic impact on the Rockefeller estate were a result of this resentment has been a subject of much historical speculation. According to Donaldson, "There is little doubt that owing to the bitter local feeling against Mr. Rockefeller at the time, the fires on his property were more numerous and serious than they might otherwise have been. Certain it is that they had to bring in train-loads of Italians to fight them, and that the unfamiliarity of the men with that kind of work made their assistance next to useless." But given Donaldson's hyperbole about "ruthless, reckless warfare on the forests," the lack of documentation for many of his assertions, his decidedly apologetic treatment of the region's wealthy residents and visitors and his apparent ambivalence toward its working class, his speculation about the culpability for the fires that devastated some of the Rockefeller estate must be taken with at least some caution.

A feud between Rockefeller and Brandon resident and Civil War veteran Oliver LaMora heightened tensions in the former lumber town. As described in the *Adirondack News* in 1902: "Saunders & Saunders, attorneys of Dickinson Center, scored quite a victory at the last term of court at Malone in the case entitled Oliver LaMora: Wm. Rockefeller v. Oliver LaMora. The case was brought to recover damages for violation of the park law of 1896, by trespassing upon his private park and taking fish from the middle branch of the St. Regis river [*sic*], which flows across his land." LaMora was found innocent because "it appears that a portion of the waters had been stocked with fish by the state at public expense." Rockefeller, referred to in the local press in 1904 as LaMora's "millionaire

This page: Second-growth white pine stands. Forest stands like these near the once-thriving lumber settlement of Brandon demonstrate the resilience of Adirondack forests. Both: *A. Egan photos.*

opponent," appealed the case against LaMora. The local Adirondack public clearly had a stake in the outcome. In 1904, the *Adirondack News* observed, "Since there are many other streams in private preserves that have been stocked by the state authorities, the outcome of the case is being anxiously awaited by many owners and fishermen." A new trial was granted, reversing the earlier decisions of the county court in Malone. While the oil and mineral tycoon, after several legal setbacks, eventually prevailed against LaMora in court, public opinion was decidedly on the side of the Civil War veteran, the judge reportedly ordering LaMora to pay a perfunctory fine of a mere eighteen cents.

In 1927, some twenty years after the affair had settled down, the *Lake Placid News* ran a front-page story on the feud between William Rockefeller and LaMora, describing LaMora as a "tall, old French-Canadian woodsman. He was poor and stubborn, and fearless…and repeatedly arrested by the Rockefeller interests and as soon as liberated went back to his outlaw game" of trespassing on Rockefeller's estate to hunt, fish and cut timber. This turned LaMora into a martyr and local, working-class folk hero and lawyers "sprang to his aid, without charge."

Despite the court's decision, the question of who owns publicly stocked fish may have backfired on Rockefeller. One offshoot of the publicity surrounding this affair was that the postmaster general ordered an investigation of the "Brandon post office matter." Since a court order had forbidden LaMora from entering Rockefeller's land, LaMora was effectively denied the right to retrieve his mail "because the post office formerly located at Brandon was now located at Bay Pond," on the Rockefeller preserve. A petition to move the post office back to Brandon from Rockefeller's Bay Pond estate was filed in Washington. The petition was apparently lost on a bureaucrat's desk then later fortuitously found—or so the story goes—and the post office was restored to Brandon "or at some nearby point outside of Mr. Rockefeller's estate that will be convenient for the people of the vicinity," according to a 1907 *Adirondack News* account. But that a single individual could at least temporarily disadvantage an entire community to the benefit of a single wealthy and influential landowner, only exacerbated local resentment toward Rockefeller and increased tensions between the remaining Brandonites and the wealthy industrialist.

Politically influential members of the same Rockefeller family were later responsible for finding other ways to assert their influence to protect and expand their interests in the Adirondacks and their peculiar sense of wilderness conservation on the backs of local communities and working-class families.

"Cacophonous Salute to Calumny"

First proposed in 1967 by the brother of Governor Nelson Rockefeller, Laurance, who at the time was chairman of both the president's Citizen Advisory Committee on Recreation and Natural Beauty and the State Council of Parks and Outdoor Recreation, the concept of an Adirondack

Mountains National Park met with immediate opposition from many of those who thought themselves most threatened by it: wealthy estate owners. In his speech to the Adirondack Mountain Club that year, Laurance Rockefeller stated that "you are well aware that the long-term hope is to buy up more inholdings within the blue line, but that even with the help of our bond issues this goal cannot be realized in the foreseeable future." As a solution, Laurance proposed an Adirondack Mountains National Park that would comprise 1.7 million acres within the blue line, with the state conveying its land within this area to the Department of the Interior's National Park Service, the federal agency that manages the country's national parks. He also recommended that "the federal government undertake an acquisition program for much of the balance" of the land in the Park and that "a partnership with the federal government could assure that those private lands which should be in public ownership are acquired," according to the *Adirondack Daily Enterprise* in 1967. This threatened private land ownership and industry within the boundaries of the proposed national park.

By the time of the debate over the creation of an Adirondack Mountains National Park, the National Park Service already had a foothold in the region. Recognized as a place of exceptional national value, the Adirondack Forest Preserve was designated a National Historic Landmark four years before Laurance Rockefeller's 1967 speech to the Adirondack Mountain Club. In its May 23, 1963 edition, the *Enterprise* downplayed the designation, devoting a single paragraph to the newly recognized National Historic Landmark declaring that "the recognition in no way affects the character of management of the Forest Preserve but is a ceremonial recognition."

But the National Historical Preservation Act of 1966 required that all federally funded projects located in a designated landmark be subject to the final approval of the Advisory Council on Historic Preservation, the body that recommends sites for recognition as federally designated landmarks, giving the National Park Service some "authority to administer historically significant federally owned properties," according to Nicholas Robinson in the *Law Journal Press*. This caused some consternation in 1977, when the region's Olympic Authority was informed that it was required to submit proposed changes to facilities to the advisory council for final approval, since federal funds were being used for construction, as reported in the *Adirondack Daily Enterprise*. Realization of the Park Service's jurisdiction over the matter did not go over well locally, lengthening the time and increasing the costs associated with the Olympic Authority project and requiring advisory council oversight of its construction. This awakened locals to yet another potential layer of bureaucracy in the Park, this time from the federal Advisory Council on Historic Preservation, for approval for everything from sewer projects to road construction—essentially any project in the preserve that was supported by federal funding. According to the *Enterprise*, when asked how the Adirondack Forest Preserve National Historic Landmark designation had come about in the first place, a representative of the advisory council declined to answer.

Laurance Rockefeller believed that an Adirondack Mountains National Park would bring prosperity to the economically forlorn region from anticipated increases in tourist visitation. Acknowledging that private property owners had expressed understandable angst that their homes and businesses would be condemned, he tried to assuage this concern by suggesting that as long as private use was consistent with the purpose of the proposed national park, there was no reason to establish a timetable for the public acquisition of private lands. He stopped short of suggesting how and by whom "consistency with park purpose" would be defined or whether such private land condemnations might eventually include the Rockefeller estate. After two years of research, on July 27, 1967, a recommendation to create an Adirondack Mountain National Park was made to Laurance Rockefeller. The report was presented to Governor Nelson Rockefeller and U.S. Department of the Interior secretary Stewart Udall three days later.

According to the study, which was requested by Laurance Rockefeller, an Adirondack Mountains National Park would include the High Peaks area, west to Cranberry Lake and Fourth Lake of the Fulton Chain of lakes, and south to Indian Lake. The authors of the study concluded that "we are convinced beyond any doubt that the Adirondacks are of National Park quality, and if established as a National Park would rate second to none," according to the *Adirondack Daily Enterprise* in a 1967 report. "It is our strong opinion that sufficient study has been made to determine that the Adirondacks are of national significance and that their establishment as a National Park is highly desirable," the report stated. The lead author of the report was Conrad L. Wirth, a noted preservationist who was a former director of the National Park Service and who a year earlier had been appointed chairman of the New York State Historic Trust by Laurance's brother Nelson. He was perhaps not the person most qualified to objectively and dispassionately assess the feasibility of creating a national park in the middle of the Adirondacks. Indeed, describing the origin of the national park idea during his speech to the Adirondack Mountain Club on October 28, 1967, Laurance recalled: "One evening last April I was standing in a parking lot in Washington talking with Connie Wirth, the former Director of the National Park Service. He is now associated with our organization as a consultant. I asked him if he thought that the Adirondacks might qualify as a National Park. His immediate response was an enthusiastic 'yes.'" Federal support for the proposed national park was apparently predetermined before the report was even concluded.

But beyond that parking lot conversation and the enthusiasm of two people who had everything to gain by the proposed designation, Laurance's Adirondack Mountains National Park concept was not met with much enthusiasm. Robert Ringlee, who was later the president of the Adirondack Mountain Club, immediately replied to Rockefeller's proposal with a position statement:

> *While we agree on the nature and seriousness of the problems, we do not believe that the proposed National Park is the best solution, for several reasons.... While the park, as proposed, might effectively prevent undesirable development of lands now privately owned, it is questioned seriously whether or not National Park status in the long-term view could offer as thorough protection of natural values of lands which are now forest preserve as can be provided by the state under constitutional safeguards. It also seems very probable that the displacement of current businesses, enterprises, and uses envisioned by the proposal would create such great pressures on the rest of the Adirondack Forest Preserve that implementation of the park proposal might mean complete destruction of the Adirondack Forest Preserve as we now know it.*

Instead, the Adirondack Mountain Club preferred other solutions, such as "control of unsuitable development by local or area zoning of private lands," a prophetic political position, as it would turn out.

But here is where the Adirondack Mountains National Park movement became interesting, reminding us of how a park concept became a reality some three-quarters of a century earlier as part of continuing efforts to create a rich man's paradise. Curiously, the William Rockefeller estate near Paul Smiths was not included in the boundary of the proposed national park. Speaking of the delineation of the proposed national park boundaries, one critic at the time stated that "the boundary line drawn on the map is surely unresearched but it is perhaps significant that certain tracts of land are excluded. The William Rockefeller holdings in the northern part of the Park are excluded, for example, and the ¼-million-acre preserve owned by the fabulously well-to-do membership of the little-known largest private property owner in the Adirondack Park, the Adirondack League Club, is also excluded…one wonders why the person who drew the map didn't include this section for appropriation and thereby include an almost equal area of presently-owned state land," as reported at the time in the *Adirondack Daily Enterprise*. Three weeks later, the editor of the *Enterprise* weighed in on Rockefeller's and the Park Service's chutzpah in some disbelief: "How could it have happened that, as the proposed national park was outlined on the map, the substantial property belonging to William Rockefeller found itself just outside the area subject to acquisition? Since two very important members of the Rockefeller family are involved in the situation, one as governor and the other as chairman of the state parks, this omission might come under the heading of 'leading with your chin.'" The newspaper's editor was James Loeb, who would later figure into the creation of a controversial alternative to an Adirondack Mountains National Park.

Among some local private property rights advocates, there was little doubt that this was more about the preservation of the Adirondacks for the wealthy than the stewardship of the region's natural resources and resource-based economies and communities. As reported in the *Enterprise* in August 1967, "Consistent with long accepted national park policy, the proposed Adirondack Mountains National Park would be a plant and animal sanctuary to permit restoration as nearly as possible of wildlife and the natural environment to the grandeur that the area possessed when frontiersmen first saw it," leaving little doubt that this was more about wilderness preservation for the few than a plan to find synergies between local communities and the natural landscapes in which they were nestled, with the actual benefits of a national park to local economies remaining very elusive. Pushback from the region's already struggling forestry sector, for example, claimed that, while timber harvesting on private Park lands and wood processing would support $9,100,000 in wages, a national park would contribute wages of only $1,900,000, according to the *Enterprise*.

James I. Loeb, former owner and editor of the *Adirondack Daily Enterprise*, described the exclusion of the Rockefeller estate at Bay Pond from the boundaries of Laurance Rockefeller's proposed Adirondack Mountains National Park as "leading with your chin." Adirondack Daily Enterprise, *1994*.

Controversy about what appeared to be the proposed national park's strategic exclusion of the estates of some wealthy part-time Adirondack residents aside, the local media appeared to be generally opposed to the national park proposal, stating that a national park would comprise "the central and most scenic portion of the original state plan. The federal government would take 1.1 million-acres of state park land and would purchase the other 600,000 privately held acres that are scattered in patches throughout the area. Five existing settlements, including the famous resorts of Lake Placid and Saranac Lake, would be retained to provide services to park visitors," the *Enterprise* reported at the time, providing a framework for a local caretaker economy indispensable to the management of Adirondack estates, as it had been since the time of Adirondack Murray.

At the request of Governor Rockefeller, the Adirondack Mountains National Park Report was analyzed by the New York State Conservation Commission, which weighed in with its own report, published in January 1968. The commission's report referred to "dramatic losses of land to timber pirates, squatters and fire" as rationales for the original creation of an Adirondack Park Forest Preserve in 1885. Among other assertions offered by the commission, the report then warned that "creation of a [Adirondack Mountains] National Park would disorganize the [forest products] industry, perhaps irretrievably." In addition, businesses related to the Park's tourism industry would also be "dislocated" within a proposed national park.

Significantly, the Conservation Commission's 1968 report to the governor noted that "in its 1962 survey, 'Parks for America,' the National Park Service recommended *against* a change in the status of the Adirondacks, noting that New York 'will undoubtedly continue, under constitutional limits, to exercise caution and judgment in the use of New York's wildlands for intensive recreation,'" essentially advocating for a status quo that would preserve the commission's authority over the Park, rather than that of the federal government's Department of the Interior. If the commission had known that after the failure of Laurance Rockefeller's national park movement the governor would respond by creating another agency as the managing authority over the Adirondack Park's preserve lands, the narrative of the commission's report may have been composed quite differently.

The Conservation Commission was also critical of the Adirondack National Park Report's erroneous estimates of the cost of the acquisition of private lands that would comprise a national park, stating that "it seems clear that the National Park report is in error when it states that 90 percent of the private land in the proposed National Park, 512,460 acres can be acquired for $51,246,000" (p. 12). Discussing the value of the timber industry to the state—"New York State benefits more from timber-based economic activities than any other state in the United States"—the commission's report estimated the total projected timber revenue of about $67,000,000 in the Park, $11,390,000 of which would derive from private lands within the proposed national park. Losses in jobs for woods workers and mill employees would also be significant, the report asserted. "The forest-based complex currently generates about $150 million of annual income for more than 15,000 people in the 12 counties directly concerned in wages, cut timber value, fuel and power, and other ancillary factors of production." The commission went on to criticize the notion of a land exchange "as a remedy to the dislocation resulting from the elimination of private forestry within the proposed National Park" as illusory, since there was not enough high-quality timberland outside of the proposed national park to compensate for that loss. The report made similar arguments for the tourism and outdoor recreation industries and the losses that would accrue to those sectors of the Park's economy by a national park designation.

Indeed, the impacts of the proposed national park on the Adirondacks' forestry sector, a major economic driver in the region that brought far better year-round wages and contributions to the region's economy than recreation and tourism, were not discussed in any detail in Laurance Rockefeller's 1967 speech, except to acknowledge that "the timber industry is at present a mainstay of the economy of the Adirondack counties" and that "I believe we can make sure that the industry is not put out of business by any [national] park," according to the *Adirondack Daily Enterprise*. However, the report made to Laurance by his friend Wirth conceded that there "would be some local loss of pulp and paper industries" due to the creation of a national park, with little or no plan for how the local communities that depended on these industries would ultimately survive a national park designation. The inference seemed to be—they wouldn't.

Laurance Rockefeller's poorly conceived attempt to create an Adirondack Mountains National Park further exposed frictions between Adirondackers and wealthy Park landowners. His 2004 obituary in the *New York Times* read this way:

> *Another controversy concerned Mr. Rockefeller's effort to have New York's huge Adirondack Park, the largest state park in the country, be put under federal control as a National Park. Starting in 1961 Mr. Rockefeller*

> *commissioned a series of studies that suggested that turning the park, which is the size of Vermont, over to the National Park Service would be the most effective way to reverse commercial incursions by timber companies and others, since federal regulations on land use were more stringent than those of the state. The opposition of local residents and politicians ultimately swamped the idea but Mr. Rockefeller's continued emphasis on the park's importance has been credited with reversing years of neglect, deterioration and exploitation as the state government asserted greater control.*

Laurance and Wirth must have been aware that federal regulations under an Adirondack Mountains National Park would have further constrained the forestry sector, despite Laurance's earlier assertions about supporting the timber industry as a "mainstay of the economies of the Adirondack counties" under their proposed national park jurisdiction.

Not going down without a fight, the Adirondack Mountains National Park movement that appeared to have lost steam for a couple of decades reemerged in the 1980s as a solution to address "economic hardships in the Park and a lack of funding to realize the state's desire to buy more land for the Forest Preserve," while others saw the renewed national park conversation as a possible "catalyst to stir the state Legislature to appropriate money without a bond act," the *Adirondack Daily Enterprise* reported in 1988. Again, the movement didn't catch on.

Despite the failure of their Adirondack Mountains National Park idea, the movement wasn't finished. Indeed, the Adirondack Park Agency, the Park's managing authority, appears to owe its roots, at least in part, to a series of ploys by a few wealthy Adirondack estate owners and duplicitous politicians seeking to shape the Adirondacks for their exclusive enjoyment. Soon after the poorly conceived national park idea had faded away due to a lack of interest, even among environmental organizations, a Temporary Study Commission of the Future of the Adirondacks (TSCFA) was appointed by Governor Nelson Rockefeller on September 19, 1968. Of the eleven people originally appointed to the TSCFA, none were full-time or longtime residents of the Adirondacks. One of the appointees was James Loeb, who was co-publisher of the *Adirondack Daily Enterprise*, spending much of his time in that position as U.S. Ambassador to Peru and Guinea. Six members of the commission were noted in the order issued by the governor's office as being from New York City.

The gist of the TSCFA's 1971 report recommended limiting development in the blue line. The study commission, strategically chaired by New

York City business executive Harold Hochschild, a vice-president of the Association for the Protection of the Adirondacks and a wealthy Blue Mountain Lake estate owner, recommended to Laurance's brother Nelson that "an independent, bipartisan Adirondack Park Agency should be created by statute with general power over the use of private land in the park." As yet another example of the clumsy politicization of the Park and the tensions between locals and wealthy Park landowners, this was viewed by one local official and Park observer this way:

> *Laurance's brother Nelson, the governor, then bailed out his brother through a classic political ploy. He appointed a study commission, "to study it to death," as the old state capitol saying goes. But his appointees instead studied into life the idea of zoning the private lands of the Adirondacks.... The agency was created and engaged in a whirlwind series of public hearings at which, as a rule, the speakers* [ed: of which the article's author was one] *told the natives how good a park plan would be for them. The natives, I suspect, were so stunned by all the uproar that they didn't get around to dumping manure on the agency grounds in Ray Brook until some time later. Then the fame of the agency was firmly secured when a young man who had been drinking in a barroom in Tupper decided to burn down its offices. He failed.*[18]

According to *The New York Times* in 1971, "The commission's report makes no fewer than 181 recommendations, requiring some time for study. But the central proposal is one that warrants unreserved immediate endorsement. It calls for establishment of 'an independent, bipartisan Adirondack Park Agency, with planning and land-use control powers over all the land in the park,'" in order to protect the Adirondacks from "the pressures of an increasingly leisure-minded population [that is] subjecting them to overuse, wrong use and plain abuse." A half century later, the ecological impacts of some "leisure-minded" tourists appear to have only worsened.

Lacking an Adirondack Mountains National Park, then, a governing authority would be installed instead, accomplishing some of the same objectives, including protecting the Adirondack estates of influential downstaters. Indeed, weighing in on the report of the TSCFA, one Adirondack environmental advocacy group described the creation of the APA as an ultimate outgrowth of Laurance Rockefeller's 1967 proposal for an Adirondack National Park.[19] From a successful attempt to establish a buffer for his estate by squeezing a once-thriving Adirondack settlement out of existence (William), to a failed attempt to create an Adirondack Mountains National Park (Laurance) that, history suggests, would have excluded the estate, followed soon after by the creation of an Adirondack Park Agency (Nelson)—the next best alternative to a federally managed national park that excluded the Rockefeller estate from federal condemnation—there was an ongoing, decades-long attempt by one wealthy and politically influential family and its allies to dominate all aspects of the Adirondack experience, leading to a consolidation and shoring up of a rich man's paradise.

On May 22, 1973, Governor Rockefeller signed bill A. 7577, placing 3.7 million acres of private land under strict zoning control by the APA. According to North Country Public Radio (NCPR) in 2013, "The Adirondack Park Land Use Development Plan, which the governor pushed through the state legislature, established new zoning rules for private land that aimed to protect open space and limit residential development," making the 6-million-acre Park the largest zoned area in the continental United States.

A decade after the governor signed the bill, in 1983, William McLaughlin, a well-known reporter and colorful columnist for the *Adirondack Daily Enterprise* and former Saranac Lake Citizen of the Year, reiterated that Governor Rockefeller's creation of the Adirondack Park Agency was a step toward creating an alternative to the failed Adirondack Mountains National Park. Both wealthy second-home owners and year-round locals had rallied against the national park idea. Quoting Governor Rockefeller's speechwriter, Joseph Persico, the columnist suggested that:

> *In 1967 as the proposal for the Adirondack National Park took wing, wealthy owners of secluded summer homes and wilderness estates or lodges "were outraged by Laurence Rockefeller's traitorous act against his class." The cacophonous salute to calumny gained strength as "humbler year-round residents of the Adirondacks saw their lives and lands falling into the clutches of federal bureaucrats."…From the moment of his brother's setback, according to Persico, Nelson began to engineer the creation of the state Adirondack Park Agency. "By 1972 he had succeeded and by 1973 he had slogged through fierce local opposition to have this new agency equipped with power to decide the future use of every plot of privately held land in the six million-acre Adirondack Park, unprecedented zoning authority for a state government."*

Referring to Nelson Rockefeller as "the Merlin of Millionaires," the governor, McLaughlin continued, "managed in his own authoritarian

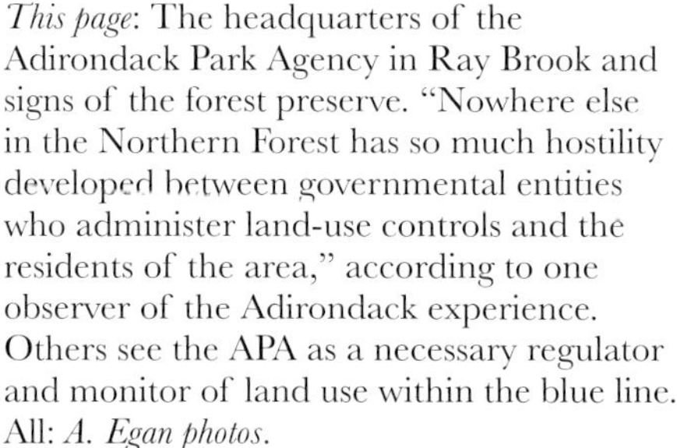

This page: The headquarters of the Adirondack Park Agency in Ray Brook and signs of the forest preserve. "Nowhere else in the Northern Forest has so much hostility developed between governmental entities who administer land-use controls and the residents of the area," according to one observer of the Adirondack experience. Others see the APA as a necessary regulator and monitor of land use within the blue line. All: *A. Egan photos.*

fashion to give Laurance a wilderness and in so doing salvaged his own conscience, if any, by arguing that hundreds of years from now Americans may still be enjoying the last great wilderness in the Northeast. It would appear in retrospect that because of Nelson's great love for and loyalty to his brother Adirondack citizens were awarded the golden anchor," a reference to the newly created Adirondack Park Agency. Laurance Rockefeller's *New York Times* obituary, published on July 12, 2004, made no mention of his failed attempt at establishing an Adirondack Mountains National Park or his plan to exclude the Rockefeller estate at Bay Pond from the proposed park's boundaries. The obituary, however, suggested that Laurance "revealed an unusual mix of ingeneousness and perhaps chutzpah when he wrote an article for *Reader's Digest* in 1976 called, 'The Case for a Simpler Life,' despite owning valuable art, many large houses and expensive automobiles, and other luxuries."

A tribute to McLaughlin posted in the *Enterprise* on January 13, 1986, on the day after his death, offered these observations, likely reflecting the feelings of resignation and powerlessness of many of the Park's year-round residents toward changes to their communities brought about by those more politically influential than they:

> *"Apathy is one of the chief enemies of the Adirondack citizen who makes his home within the park on a year-round basis. The heavy downstate vote factor leaves him with little to fight with and he relies heavily on God and common sense to save him from the tentacles of the state octopus now encircling his home and his future," McLaughlin wrote shortly after the Park Agency's inception in the early 1970's....He never gave in. In 1983, he added this observation about the natives' plight under Agency law: "We may be playing a losing game but we are playing it with a relish and a will to survive. We bear well the crushing mandates that have been heaped upon us in the same manner as the Forever Wild anvil was clamped to our unsuspecting shoulders back in the cobweb era."*

The failed attempt to strategically convert some of the Adirondack Park to an Adirondack Mountains National Park and the subsequent creation of the Adirondack Park Agency were not the end of efforts by influential people from outside the Park to further define the Adirondacks, the Adirondack experience and the well-being—and now more uncertain future—of Adirondack communities.

Blue Lines and Green Lines

A 1988 land sale by Diamond International Corporation of some one million mostly forested acres in Maine, New Hampshire, Vermont and New York—some for development—incited legitimate concerns about forest conservation across the region. The region comprising these and contiguous lands was dubbed the Northern Forest, and a study was commissioned by Congress to look at the region as a single political entity, charging the U.S. Forest Service to work with the states to look at forest ownership patterns and utilization. One outcome of this initiative was the creation of the Northern Forest Lands Council in 1990, made up of representatives from all four states charged to work together and further investigate issues related to the disposition of the Northern Forest and to make recommendations to Congress and the states. The council released thirty-seven draft recommendations in 1994 under the title *Finding Common Ground: Conserving the Northern Forest*, "designed to maintain traditional patterns of land ownership in the Northern Forest."[20]

This would include creating a Northern Forest Research Cooperative that would investigate ecosystem health, forest management and economic development; develop a state-managed public land acquisition planning process; fund land acquisition projects; protect wilderness; and provide the region with federal land conservation dollars.

A year later, a Northern Forest Stewardship Act enjoyed bipartisan political support across the four Northern Forest states, with the Adirondack Park considered by some to be a model for a multistate forest stewardship partnership. "As the country's most prominent attempt at 'greenlining' (the practice of defining a region in which special land-use regulations and programs apply, an approach used widely in Europe but in only a few places in the United States) the Adirondack Park had been mentioned early on as a possible model for the 26-million-acre Northern Forest study area," according to one observer.[21] Not everyone saw it that way, however. Although the U.S. Senate passed the Northern Forest Stewardship Act (S.1163), the House version (HR 2421) became stuck in the Rules Committee, chaired by Representative Gerald Solomon, whose upstate New York district included Finch, Pruyn and Company, a paper company that, at the time, employed hundreds of workers, according to the *Adirondack Daily Enterprise* in 1996. Finch, Pruyn, the second-largest private landowner in the Adirondack Park at the time, was accused of scuttling the act and backstabbing supporters of the legislation by suggesting that any land acquisitions in the Park be carried out according to plans conceived by the state.

Despite its demise as a political land management construct, there are those who continue to refer to the region as the Northern Forest. Some scientists, for example, study the place as if it were socially, economically and ecologically homogeneous, despite significant differences in these attributes across the region. Indeed, the Adirondack Park's unique history, geology, and human, landscape and local ecology—not to mention its unique land-use regulations and administration—suggest that it be disaggregated from northern Vermont, New Hampshire and Maine in discussions about a northern forest region.

In the end, there was little local support for a Northern Forest. The Northern Forest Stewardship Act was specific in stating that "states must work in partnership with local and Federal Government" and that "people must appreciate that the Northern Forest has values that are important beyond the boundaries of the forest," perhaps raising suspicions of a loss of local control over the disposition of lands located within the Northern Forest region, an increase in federal government oversight and the possible creation of a Northern Forest National Park that reawakened concerns about a similar concept introduced, then abandoned, in the Adirondacks in the 1960s.

Whatever one's position on the Northern Forest idea, there appeared to be justifiable angst among locals. Despite language in the act that asserted "the rights of private owners" and "continuous flow of timber, pulpwood, and other forest products," these fears were likely exacerbated by language in the act that suggested that "the Secretary of Agriculture, acting through the Chief of the Forest Service, and the Secretary of the Interior, acting through the Director of the Park Service and Director of the United States Fish and Wildlife Service, at the request of the State of Maine, New Hampshire, Vermont or New York, shall provide technical and financial assistance for land acquisition planning and land acquisition." These federal agencies manage National Forests, National Parks and Wildlife Refuges, respectively—all having a vested interest in adding acreage over which they would exert land-use management authority. In addition, emerging from a failed attempt to create a national park in the Adirondacks, but having a foothold in the region given the designation of the Forest Preserve as a National Historic Landmark, the Park Service in particular would seem primed to reinvigorate the national park discussion, but from a position of greater involvement in land acquisition and control that would have been supported by federal legislation.

Citing a lack of economic opportunity and too many restrictions, private property–rights advocates spoke out against the Northern Forest Lands Council and the APA, perhaps most notably at a heated meeting in the Adirondacks in 1994. While the "ferocity" of the objections to the greenlining plans articulated by the Northern Forest Lands Council "was unique to New York,"[22] not all states in the region were on board. "Centralized planning may be considered by many as successful, but for the rural landowner and worker it is usually devastating," wrote one Vermont opinion leader, referring to the idea of land-use regulation in the Northern Forest similar to that found within the blue line. "We need only look at the Adirondack Park to see what can occur. Nowhere else in the Northern Forest has so much hostility developed between governmental entities who administer land-use controls and the residents of the area. People see their property rights more and more limited, and they resent the continued use of public funds to buy land that will be forever removed from the production of commodities."[23]

According to a proponent of the Northern Forest concept from Vermont, representatives from Maine, a state with significant acreage in industrial forests in its northern counties, blocked "every attempt to designate any form of 'green line,' recommend public land acquisition other than for small tracts of significant natural areas, or to establish an interstate commission with any effective authority....With Maine lands being the bulk and heart of the Northern Forest, there seemed to be no way to move ahead without support of that state's leadership."[24] In addition, according to the same observer, "theatrical exchanges" by private property–rights advocates during Northern Forest Lands Study hearings in New York and Vermont, sometimes targeting the Adirondack Park Agency, appeared, in part, to reflect reactions to private forest regulations within the Park.

According to an article published in the *Adirondack Daily Enterprise* in 1997, Adirondack property-rights advocates saw the Northern Forest Stewardship Act as initiating "the creation of a federal land 'empire' in the North Country" that would represent another in a long line of attempts by those outside the Park to further preserve the Adirondacks, benefiting wealthy out-of-state Adirondack landowners and disadvantaging local, often marginalized, Park residents. Adirondackers were not alone in their concerns. Residents of the Northern Forest region, in general, had serious issues with the proposed designation. Overall, residents of the multistate region felt disconnected economically from the forests that dominate the region's landscape. Importantly, two-thirds of these residents did not believe that low-wage, seasonal recreation and tourism, rather than forestry and agriculture, should be the foundation for their local economies, a sentiment that was especially strong in the Adirondacks.

The question of the intended size of the Adirondack Park remains a source of tension among longtime Park residents, local governments, regulators, the state and those who continue to advocate for a distinct, regionally managed Northern Forest that includes the Adirondacks. Yet despite strong opposition to additional public-land acquisitions by citizens of the Northern Forest region—and particularly among Adirondackers who understood regional administration and land-use control better than residents of other states in the region—"The [Northern Forest Lands] Council supported increased land acquisition funding at both the state and federal level to meet this need" to acquire lands of exceptional ecological, recreational, and cultural value "(while) seeking ways for Maine, New Hampshire, Vermont and New York to maintain the 'traditional patterns of land ownership and use' of the Northern Forests."[25] This only served to amplify concerns that the Northern Forest Lands program was an attempt to transfer land from the private sector to government ownership and to create a multistate land-use control agency modeled after the Adirondack Park Agency.

Despite falling short politically, the notion of a Northern Forest as a single ecological, social and economic region has persisted among many of its initial supporters. Recent references to the Northern Forest suggest an area of twenty-six million acres spread over thirty-four counties in the Northern Forest region, with a total population of approximately 2.3 million people, less than 130,000 of whom live in the six-million-acre Adirondack Park. While there have been recent reports of "modest" population gains in the Northern Forest overall,[26] growth has been spotty and concentrated around areas near Burlington, Vermont, and along the southern edge of the Northern Forest region most proximate to the Boston metropolitan area, while the Adirondack Park has been steadily losing population. A 2012 study found that "population gains were greatest in recreational areas and least in manufacturing areas."[27] However, it's unclear if the decline in population in these areas was a result of the steep decline in manufacturing in the region generally, and, perhaps most especially in the Adirondacks.

The Beauty Pageant

Tensions around the designation and administration of a Northern Forest appeared to echo concerns expressed by many Adirondackers over the creation of the 9.9-million-acre Champlain-Adirondack Biosphere Reserve (CABR) a few years earlier in 1989. The CABR was described as "an ecology program aimed at conserving biological resources," according to a report in the *Adirondack Daily Enterprise* in 1989. Encompassing the entire Adirondack Park and the Lake Champlain watershed, including much of western Vermont and the Green Mountain National Forest, it is the largest biosphere reserve in North America, with a human population exceeding that of any biosphere reserve in the world. Indeed, the Adirondack Forest Preserve was considered by some to be the "core protected area" of the CABR.[28] Despite assertions from UNESCO reported in the *Enterprise* that the designation "imposes no regulatory restrictions or binding legal obligations on its biosphere reserves," as in the case of the attempt to create a Northern Forest, there was significant grassroots opposition to the CABR, with some claiming that Adirondack residents and local government officials were unaware that they had been nominated for reserve status until the official designation was first reported to Adirondack residents in the *Adirondack Daily Enterprise* on May 1, 1989. The CABR is the fourth-largest such reserve in the world and the largest in a settled area. "It's not a legal designation with constraints. There's no international treaty involved," according to National Park Service spokesman William Greg in the *Glens Falls Post-Star* in 1989. According to a spokesperson for the APA in the same article, "the states are planning to establish an organization to oversee research, demonstration projects, training and education in the reserve." So far, there is little evidence that a cohesive, functioning organization has ever existed.

While there was an early effort in 1990 in the Adirondacks to develop educational programming relating to the region as a Biosphere Reserve, little appears to have become of that project, and subsequent efforts to exploit the designation for education and research have been somewhat muted. "Not many people understand the global significance of the Champlain-Adirondack Biosphere Reserve," asserted the assistant director of the Visitors Interpretive Center in Paul Smiths, where the group of educators from New York, Vermont and Quebec met. "Once we started talking about the educational opportunities the reserve presents, the educators became enthusiastic about working on programs for primary and secondary schools within and beyond the biosphere," the *Enterprise* reported. However, the CABR's "global significance"—much less any sense of local significance—appears to have existed somewhere along the continuum from elusive to illusory.

Symptomatic of the rather clandestine and top-down formulation and consummation of the designation, referencing the CABR in 2002 in a discussion about climate change in the Adirondacks, the *Adirondack Daily Enterprise* reported that "the United Nations' Man and the Biosphere Program declared the Adirondack/Lake Champlain region to be a World Biosphere Reserve, recognizing the global importance of its forests and waters as well as the efforts made to ensure environmental protection." The unfortunate, operative verb being "declared," with no mention of a partnership between the UN and the people who were year-round residents of the Park.

When Adirondackers, smarting from earlier attempts to create an Adirondack Mountains National Park, first heard about the designation, the leader of the Citizens Council of the Adirondacks claimed at a meeting of the Champlain-Adirondack Biosphere Reserve Committee that "the biosphere designation is part of a larger, perhaps international, 'elitist' plan to impose stricter zoning regulations on beautiful areas throughout the world," to which a committee representative suggested that the designation "is purely for academic and scientific research, and has nothing to do with regulations," reported Laura Rappaport of the *Enterprise* in 1990. However, several years later, after the cancelation of a meeting related to the biosphere designation because of fears of disruption by those who supported private-property rights, a proponent of the CABR from the University of Vermont tried to make the case for the designation based not on its research value but rather on regional economics, asserting that it would enhance tourism. However, a 2020 search of the official state of Vermont tourism website revealed no reference to a Biosphere Reserve, nor was there reference to the CABR on the official Adirondack tourism website, calling into question both the motivations behind the UVM professor's assertion and his unfulfilled claims about the value of the designation to the region's tourism industry.

Nevertheless, concerns expressed by Adirondack citizens about the CABR were called absurd by the UVM academic, who compared the designation to "winning the Miss America pageant," asserting that it was no more than an honorary designation that recognized the importance of the region as a means of promoting its culture and resources. The benefit of the CABR, then, had morphed from its potential research value, to its promise of economic development, to simply an honorary award. Apparently speaking for the entire state, the UVM prof claimed that Vermont is using the designation to promote the region and enhance tourism, asserting that "as far as Vermont is concerned, we're proud of the designation. If (New York) doesn't want it, we'll take it," according to an *Adirondack Daily Enterprise* article by staff writer Matthew Russell in 1993. However, questioning the professor's assertion of the innocuous intent of the designation to residents of the Adirondacks, the *Enterprise* report cautioned that "legislation to recognize the designation includes references to the use of information about the biosphere region to develop "management" plans for the region through existing planning processes and agencies."

Indeed, there appears to have been at least some justification for being cautious. The Madrid Action Plan for Biosphere Reserves for the period 2008–13, for example, states that it aims "to raise biosphere reserves to be the principle internationally-designated areas dedicated to sustainable development in the 21st century," but it stops short of defining what it means by "sustainable development." The plan goes on to articulate a goal of "linking global environmental agendas to national and local development aspirations...guided not only by the community most directly involved in managing biosphere reserves, but also by the broader community inspired by the concept and experimenting with it." The degree to which truly local input would be encouraged, gathered and then actually used in decision-making processes going forward was unclear. Also unclear is the definition of "broader community" and the influence it may have on the lives and livelihoods of Adirondack residents.

Citizens of the Adirondack Park were not alone in their skepticism about a Biosphere Reserve designation. Quoting the executive director of a governor's council for the state of Minnesota, who related his experiences from a similar biosphere designation proposal in his state, the alliance chairman related to the *Enterprise* in 1993: "What really alarmed us…is the lack of public information and lack of public participation by those that would be most impacted by it. These places including the one you're talking about in New York and Vermont were nominated without anybody knowing about it. We find that absolutely unbelievable in a Democracy." He continued, "As a result of the council's findings, the state of Minnesota recommended withdrawal of the nomination which the Department of State did." It is worth noting that, when local citizens have been involved in the vetting process for Biosphere Reserve designation elsewhere in New York State, there has been broad opposition to the concept. For example, when the Catskill Mountain region was nominated for this designation in 1994, five years after the CABR was announced, the application was eventually withdrawn from consideration in large part due to local outcry against the idea. Again, the public appeared to have been brought into the conversation very late in a process that had been initiated at the planning stages in 1986, creating resentment and raising suspicions about the intent and potential ramifications of the designation.

While in the short term the non-inclusive approach to the creation of the CABR might have been considered successful, in the longer term the concept failed from a lack of regional recognition and implementation, especially in the Adirondacks. Indeed, the lack of clarity as to its meaning and significance to regional ecosystems and local communities appeared to be a key reason for its ultimate marginalization. For better or worse, indications are that the Biosphere Reserve as an operational construct, at least in the Adirondacks, simply fizzled out. It's an idea that has become less relevant now than it was in 1990 or perhaps than it might have been if there had not been considerable pushback from local Park residents and if they had been involved in the process from the beginning, rather than having the CABR imposed on them seemingly overnight. Tensions around the CABR were as much a symptom of the perception of Adirondack residents that Park policies were being driven by outsiders determining the disposition of the Park's quality of life; poor communication between locals and the state's agencies and elected officials; a lack of transparency in decision-making; and continuing conflict between preservationists and conservationists fed by often storified historical threads of forest destruction and the marginalization of the region's working class.

Years later, some continue to embrace the elusive value of the CABR designation. Discussing the rationale behind the designation, one observer wrote: "International recognition of the ecological and social importance of this region through UNESCO's Man and the Biosphere (MAB) program supported the creation of the Lake Champlain Basin Program and the Northern Forest Lands Project." Then lamenting the missed opportunity that the CABR, as well as other Biosphere Reserves in the United States, represented, he asserted that "beyond these significant initial side-effects, nothing more has since come of it. The CABR and the 46 other designated Biosphere Reserves (BRs) in America all failed to become truly functional, deleting America's potentially important contribution from the global effort to protect biodiversity, promote research, monitoring and information exchange, and demonstrate the development of sustainable communities."[29] Of the designation process, the author goes on to state that "Our failure, since 1991, to nominate additional BRs and the loss of fully functioning already-designated BRs like the CABR may ultimately be the result of a political backlash against a top-down, paternal, perhaps even elitist, coercive Command and Control approach to solving environmental and social problems so popular in the 60s and 70s." Given its surprise unveiling, astonishing lack of public input and subsequent local pushback, there is little doubt that this was the case for the CABR.

Top-down, paternalistic, elitist, coercive. From its creation and its expansion, to policies related to its economy, its ecology and its society, these words have often been used or implied in the ongoing dialog and persistent polemics around the disposition of the Adirondack Park; an unsuccessful attempt to establish an Adirondack Mountains National Park and the subsequent creation of a land-use management authority in the Adirondack Park Agency; a National Historic Landmark designation whose implications and costs took the region's Olympic Authority, among others, by surprise; a failed movement to institute a regionally managed Northern Forest that would include the Adirondacks; and a Biosphere Reserve designation that didn't deliver on promises of economic development—all of these have contributed to both a wariness among Adirondackers toward land-use controls and the evolution of a rich man's paradise comfortably nestled in the resource-rich north country of New York that is home to some of the state's poorest families and communities.

4

POIGNANT RURAL POVERTY

Here is where poverty makes its home.
—A. Balagtas, "The Low-profile Poor," 1988

Low-Profile Poor

Raw income data do not always reflect the reality of day-to-day rural poverty in a place like the Adirondack Park, where regulations have increased costs, manufacturing jobs have dwindled, wealthy second-home owners have driven up the cost of housing and land and transportation networks—and therefore access to essential services—are limited. "There is nothing Appalachian about rural poverty in northern New York," according to one historian. "Living poor is as widespread and inveterate an Adirondack condition as the distortion or denial of that condition in the public record."[30] According to one observer of the Adirondack experience, "Besides high poverty rates, the Adirondacks also have some of the highest unemployment rates in the state. In 2000, when the United States had an unemployment rate of 4.1 percent, 22 Adirondack towns had unemployment rates of over 10 percent and six had rates of over 15 percent....For too many Adirondackers there is not enough work to go around."[31] And much of the work that is available is in low-wage, often seasonal and unpredictable service-sector jobs related to tourism and hospitality.

Unfortunately for the Park's permanent residents, given the relatively low population density and dwindling voter base in the Adirondacks, it likely makes

This page: Adirondack hard times. The Park's "poignant rural poverty" has been dismissed by some as no worse than that of other rural places. Others see rural poverty as the Park's "biggest challenge." *Both from A. Egan photos.*

more sense politically to focus on alleviating poverty in the state's more populated urban areas. In the meantime, because of poor transportation networks in the Park, Adirondackers will continue to travel "long distances for jobs, groceries, health care and social service programs"[32]—stark realities that don't emerge from data related to what has been described by a former commissioner of the New York State Department of Environmental Conservation in the Adirondack Daily Enterprise in 1975 as the Adirondacks' "poignant rural poverty."

The Park's unique zoning restrictions further constrain the quality of life of local residents. "The early results indicate that lot-size requirements and other APA regulations to protect the environment have driven housing costs up to a point where many people trying to purchase a primary home in the area can't afford it, creating a housing crisis. Secondary home purchases are not being affected to the same extent," according to a report in the *Glens Falls Post-Star* in 1989. This tension between Park residents and those "from away" is an underlying theme in the Park, often resulting in the resentment of longtime local residents toward wealthier, more influential, seasonal, second-home owners, replaying the adversarial relationships that, according to some, likely led to retributive arson that resulted in some of the most catastrophic Adirondack wildfires of the late nineteenth and early twentieth centuries, as well as local pushback against top-down political initiatives such as a Biosphere Reserve, a national park and a northern forest.

The region's loss of much of its manufacturing, combined with its poor transportation networks, have had impacts on the small hamlets once supported by resource extraction and manufacturing. A headline in the *Plattsburg Press Republican* in the fall of 1989 read, "Adirondacks Boasts Its Fair Share of Ghost Towns," generally associated with the decline of the mining industry and the loss of most of the region's lumber and pulp industries. Indeed, the 1990 Commission on the Adirondacks in the Twenty-first Century found that:

- Incomes in Adirondack Park towns were below both the state average and incomes in other rural areas of the state. Importantly, given the sparse populations of many Adirondack towns, a few wealthy residents can skew the average income significantly.
- Families in counties in the Adirondack Park had lower incomes than the statewide average at the time of the 1980 census. This was especially true in Franklin and Hamilton Counties.
- Only 24.2 percent of persons aged twenty-five or older who live in Park towns had at least one year of college in 1980, compared with

36.0 percent for non-Park rural counties and 32.2 percent for the state. Indeed, none of the Adirondack Park counties exceeded the non-Park rural counties in this regard.

- During this period, Adirondack Park employment was primarily in the low-paying service and public sectors. The natural resource extraction sector—including agriculture, forestry and mining—was less important in the Park than in "comparable rural counties," primarily due to the "lack of adaptability" of the Park's agriculture sector and the "phasing out" of most of the Park's mining industry.

Some twenty years later, census data from 2010 indicated that "the collective population of the towns and villages wholly within the Adirondack Park plunged over the last decade, while communities bisected by the Blue Line grew....The 70 towns and villages that lie entirely within the park collectively lost 1,848 residents, dropping the segment's total population to 127, 904. In contrast, the 31 towns and two villages only partially inside the park added 5,294 residents, a 4 percent growth—double the statewide growth trend." The report continues: "Environmental groups argue that because of the nearly 3 million-acres of off-limits state Forest Preserve, the Adirondack economy is stronger than other rural areas and the outdoor tourist economy is actually drawing people in." However, local governments countered that restrictive zoning regulations in the Park "choke out private investment and industry—creating an almost entirely taxpayer-funded population of teachers, plow truck drivers and state regulators," according to Jon Alexander and Jon Davenport in their 2011 *Post-Star* report on the Adirondack Park's population. Significantly for the future of the Park, the *Post-Star* article reported that "the Adirondack resident is significantly older, less educated and poorer than the average New York state citizen and the region is hemorrhaging youth." Despite the more optimistic interpretations and spinnings of these census data by others, it seems undeniable that unfavorable trends in population, age, income and education in the Adirondack Park predict a potentially irreversible dilemma, unless one's ultimate goal is the social, economic and demographic impoverishment of the Adirondacks.

In 2009, the Adirondack Park Regional Assessment Project (APRAP) highlighted some of the region's economic and social challenges, including a poorly diversified economy, an aging population and steep declines in school enrolments. The assessment, which surveyed eighty-five Adirondack town supervisors and mayors, as well as highway superintendents, water/

wastewater operators, fire chiefs and school superintendents, was reported by the *Albany Times Union* in 2014. Key findings include the following:

- Government-sector jobs accounted for more than 30 percent of all employment in Hamilton, Essex, Lewis and Washington Counties.
- In 2007, an estimated 44 percent of employees worked in the public sector in Franklin County. These jobs do not include employment in public education.
- The regional economy is highly dependent on correctional services, and one of every twenty-six people counted as living in the Adirondack Park resided in a correctional facility.
- Park residents averaged just under forty-three years of age, older than any state for median age. If current population trends hold, the Park's population will drop to 115,000 by 2030, which is about how many people lived in the Adirondacks during the early 1970s, when the median age of Park residents was thirty-one. The median age of Park residents is projected to be fifty-one by 2030.
- By 2020, only the west coast of Florida will exceed the Adirondacks as the oldest region in America.
- Historical references to employment in the Adirondacks note the high levels of employment that existed among the mineral-extraction and logging industries located in the Park. Bureau of Labor Statistics data indicate that employment in the category "Forestry, Logging" for the twelve counties comprising the Park fell from 467 in 2001 to 420 in 2007.
- Within the Park, employment trends showed increases in the public sector (government and education) and health services. Private-sector jobs were in decline, and season unemployment was notably higher in Adirondack counties, particularly during winter months.

But not everyone was sympathetic. Indeed, one critic of the study referred to APRAP's interpretations as "spurious" and "misleading."[33] Acknowledging that the overall population of the Park is declining and that "Adirondack demographics are less than cheerful"—especially among young families with children—while the median age of Park residents is increasing, he suggested that these trends are not unique to the Adirondacks but characterized much of small-town rural New York. He also accused the APRAP report of supporting "a dubious political agenda," apparently critical of the project's focus on soliciting input from the people who are full-time residents, public servants and municipal managers of the Park's rural communities. Comparing poverty rates among some non-Adirondack towns, he cited worse levels of poverty in Chatauqua County (located outside of the Park on the western edge of the state), for example, asserting that "conservation" should not be blamed for poverty, but rather that high poverty levels are more likely related to a place's distance from large urban centers. The author's position—that demographically the Adirondack Park is like the rest of rural America—appears to argue against the Adirondacks as a model for anything, including social and economic diversity and resilience. After all, the argument would logically go, it is no better or worse than other rural places. So, what is the value of its designation as a Park and the associated layers of land-use management authority and control, especially to the region's year-round residents? About the notion that high poverty levels are more a function of a place's distance from an urban center, census data indicate that some of the highest poverty rates in the state are in New York City, one might argue.

The argument also ignores that some in the environmental community in the Adirondacks have repeatedly opposed efforts to protect scores of jobs in the region through land swaps between the private sector and the Park. One example is the 2013 proposed land swap of two hundred acres in the Jay Mountain Wilderness with fifteen hundred acres of forestland owned by NYCO Minerals Inc. Proponents of the swap asserted that it would help sustain mineral extraction next to the wilderness for another forty years while providing the forest preserve with equivalent land elsewhere in addition to the mined land once mineral extraction was completed and the land restored. This would seem to be a win-win proposition, creating much-needed employment and supporting community stability in and proximate to the Park. But some environmental interests opposed the deal in principle, ignoring the potential benefits to local community development. Using their own nuanced definitions of ecological communities, such as old-growth forests and vernal pools, environmental groups appeared to be reaching in their attempts to stop any economic development in the preserve. Weighing in on the matter, Environmental Conservation commissioner Joe Martens stated, "Poverty may be the biggest challenge in the Adirondack Park, and if communities cannot find ways to make a living, then the park experience will fail," as reported in a 2013 article on Timesunion.com. A constitutional amendment allowing the exchange was approved by voters in November 2013, perhaps signaling some realization in Albany of the need for a better balance between preservation and local economic development.

Based on the results of the 2010 census, indicating an overall loss of population among counties wholly or partially located within the blue line, it is difficult to argue that population trends in the Park are heading in the right direction. While those in support of stringent environmental regulations have emphasized that populations have grown in ten of the twelve Adirondack counties, albeit primarily in border counties where most population growth has been in municipalities located outside the blue line, those interests aligning more closely with encouraging economic development see a further erosion of community vitality and employment growth beyond low-wage, often seasonal employment related to tourism.

Even what remained of the Northern Forest Lands Council, in its 2005 "Final Report" sponsored by the North East State Foresters Association, acknowledged that "The region's timber-based economies can be further advanced if investments in additional value-added manufacturing facilities augment the current export of the region's raw materials." Nowhere else in the so-called Northern Forest was this more true than in the Adirondack Park, which has routinely behaved as though it were a developing country in its propensity for exporting raw material outside the Park to be manufactured into wood pellets, lumber, furniture and flooring, then importing many of those forest-based products back into the Park for local consumption.

Caretaker Economy

As was the case during Adirondack Murray's time, much of the Park's economy has relied on jobs related to providing services for the region's visitors: great-camp and estate owners and their families, tourists, recreationists and, by the 1960s and '70s, prisoners. While there are still those who consider themselves "caretakers" for wealthy Adirondack landowners and their estates—and, at least locally, this can be a significant source of employment—many of the essential caretaker functions of the past are now accomplished by a dwindling population of local independent contractors and service providers. The caretaker profession is said to have evolved from that of guiding, and many

Above and opposite: Boathouse, 1886, and dining room, 1906, at the Birch Island "great camp" on Upper St. Regis Lake. Referring to the Adirondack "great camp" phenomenon of the period, a headline in the *New York Times* on June 15, 1911, read, "Camps along the St. Regis Chain of Lakes now the Goal of the City Folk—Recent Arrivals." Boathouse: *Helen Phelps Stokes photo in* Camp Chronicles, *p. 38;* dining room: *from* Stokes Records, *vol. III, after p. 128.*

current caretakers are also skilled outdoorsmen. According to one local historian writing for the *Adirondack Daily Enterprise* in 1987, Murray's rush was so "successful" that the influx of his followers far outnumbered the available number of qualified guides. As a result, the Adirondacks apparently ran out of qualified guides, encouraging pretenders to step forward to claim the profession. Verplanck Colvin helped establish the Adirondack Guides' Association in 1891 to protect their interests, and a fixed rate of pay of three dollars per day plus expenses was established. Soon, however, wealthy tourists and "sports" would decide to buy land in the Adirondacks and build their own private, lakefront great camps instead. "They could bring their families and entertain guests during the summer months and have the luxury of a comfortable hunting lodge in the fall," according to one local historian. "No more sleeping in bark shanties. Together with the main camp there would be a guide house, an ice house, and a boat house and suddenly a new occupation was born. It was a natural and simple transition to switch positions from that of guide to that of caretaker."

Not surprisingly, there were often tensions between the wealthy estate owners from away and locals employed to take care of them. "A lot of them really let you know that because they had a little money they were better than you were," according to one writer of the Adirondack caretaker

Employees of The Rocks "great camp" on Upper St. Regis Lake, circa 1920. *Adirondack Experience.*

experience.[34] However, not all such relationships were acrimonious. A more complementary description of the caretaking experience at Bay Pond, reported in the *New York Times* in the early 1900s, went like this: "Workmen and guides who have come in contact with Mr. Rockefeller at Bay Pond say that his philanthropy and charity take the form of the employment of men at clean, decent tasks at good wages. The men who work for Mr. Rockefeller breakfast at 6 A.M., go to work at 6:30, stop for the midday meal at 11:30, and cease work at 5 P.M. They have the comforts and conveniences of modern quarters, and the quality of food served to all workmen is of the best, often including the luxuries of the market."

Nevertheless, continued tensions between year-round residents and the region's tourists and second-home owners searching for refuge in the Park have surfaced periodically. In the midst of the 2020 coronavirus pandemic, for example, the headlines of the *Adirondack Daily Enterprise* proclaimed: "Counties: Don't come here," referring to the Adirondack's Franklin and Essex Counties, which at the time had six confirmed cases of the virus between them, according to reporting by Elizabeth Izzo on March 26 of that year. During the busy Memorial Day weekend a couple of months later, some visitors to the Adirondacks were greeted by a small, but vocal, protest group referring to itself as "We the People of the Adirondacks" and displaying signs that read "YOUR'RE WELCOME…TO GO HOME" and "TURN AROUND, TAKE THE VIRUS BACK DOWN." Despite the ongoing pandemic, during its apex, some parking areas at trailheads in the High Peaks were again overflowing as if it were a normal holiday weekend.

Early on, some year-round Adirondack residents and elected officials welcomed the influx of those escaping the pandemic primarily from the New York metro area, pointing out that many are Adirondack second-home owners and taxpayers, seasonal friends and neighbors who contribute to local communities and economies. Others were much more cautious. Franklin and Essex County officials issued a directive aimed at encouraging social distancing and self-quarantining to stem the spread of the virus. "To date we have seen an alarming influx of travelers from outside the county who are staying at second homes and short-term rentals," according to a release from the Essex County Board of Supervisors, which asked people to stay away from the Adirondacks during the crisis. Addressing travel to the Park by second-home owners and those staying at short-term rentals in the region, officials from the two Adirondack counties advised, "While you may be seeking refuge from the larger amount of cases downstate, you must be aware that this is a global pandemic." Officials also pointed out the strain that would be placed on the local healthcare system by such an influx, especially during a late winter–early spring shoulder season that may not be geared up for an unanticipated arrival of people from outside the Park. Referencing "non-essential travel coming into the area" as a result of the pandemic, the mayor of Lake Placid bluntly asserted that "there's no reason to come here right now," while an official with the town of Wilmington (also in Essex County) encouraged vacation rental owners to temporarily stop taking reservations. Making a distinction between refugees from New York City and Westchester County, considered epicenters of coronavirus infection in the United States at the time, and "regular people" in his Adirondack community, a local mayor urged visitors from downstate to self-quarantine for fourteen days before going to the market or other public places. "It's not to be offensive, it's just common decency," he said, according to Peter Crowley and Griffin Kelly in a March 2020 article in the *Enterprise*. Tensions and resentments were no doubt exacerbated by the assertion made by Essex County's public health director in December 2020 that tourism helped to spread COVID-19 to the Adirondack region, more emphatically laying some blame for a spike in infections in the county on careless visiting recreationists. A likely longer-term outcome of the pandemic will be the pursuit of more second homes in the Adirondacks as sanctuaries from inevitable future public-health and safety crises, further straining the ability of locals to maintain their already precarious place in the Park.

Prison Boom and Bust

While the public sector has been a major driver of much of the Park's economy, the region's heavy reliance on public employment has been extremely tenuous. Take the prison system, until a few years ago a significant employer in the region. The Adirondack prison economy boomed in the 1970s, with changes in state laws that resulted in drug offenders being sentenced to mandatory minimum sentences. The state's prison population swelled from some twenty thousand in 1959, when Governor Rockefeller took office, to almost seventy-three thousand by 2000. "As it turned out, the Rockefeller drug laws—which included tough penalties for marijuana use—would rival the land-use regulations in their impact on the Adirondacks," according to a report by Brian Mann in 2013.

To accommodate this growth, much of the additional prison space was built in northern New York, including in the Adirondacks, since land for prison infrastructure was cheaper than what could be found in and near New York City, and the state's Department of Corrections soon became the region's largest employer in an area where good-paying jobs with benefits were scarce due to the steady decline in the Park's natural-resource extraction and manufacturing sectors. At one time, one of every twenty-six Adirondack residents was a prisoner. According to Mann, "Before the Park's prison-construction boom abated in the late 1990s, about twenty state and federal correctional facilities would be operating in the Adirondacks or within a short drive of the Blue Line. New York's Corrections Department would emerge as the region's single largest employer, hiring thousands of prison guards and civilian employees, usually in much-prized middle-class jobs." Likening the Adirondack region to Siberia, Mann reported that New York State rushed to build new prisons in the Adirondack region in response to a sharp increase in drug-related crime, primarily in the New York City metro region, "converting towns that relied on logging, mining, and tourism for their prosperity into one of the largest prison complexes in the United States." The Park represented a region where prisons could be built more cheaply, as well as a remote place to which criminals could be exiled. The Adirondacks was also a region that was depressed economically, as many forest products and mining companies found operating in the Park too costly. However, the system was criticized by some prison-reform advocates as immoral—"You're locking up people in order to provide other people jobs"—and by some environmentalists as despoiling the pristine Adirondack landscape in the name of local economic development and job creation. Nevertheless, New York's Siberia was thriving. But it didn't last.

Plummeting crime rates, a politically motivated shift in prison policy that resulted in fewer incarcerations for drug-related crimes and a severe downturn in the state's economy collided in the early 2000s, resulting in a

This page: The Adirondack hamlet of Lyon Mountain and remains of the ironworks. At its peak in the 1880s, Lyon Mountain had more than 3,500 residents; the 2010 census counted 423. The mines closed in 1967 and the still-vacant Lyon Mountain Correctional Facility (*left midground*) closed in 2011, leaving many Adirondackers out of work. Both: *A. Egan photos*.

contraction of the region's prison industry, starting with the prison in Lyon Mountain, an economically depressed and geographically isolated former mining town with few other prospects. While millions of state dollars were saved by these closures, rural towns that depended almost entirely on a prison economy found themselves reeling, and the assets that were built to provide prison space were left vacant or sold for a fraction of their previous value. Governor Mario Cuomo referred to the gradual closure of many of the state's prisons as "reducing the madness of an incarceration society," according to an NCPR report by Natasha Haverty in 2014. What he neglected to plan for was an alternative source of employment for the many working-class Adirondackers who were employed by the state's prison system and living in a park with little economic diversity and resilience, resulting in severe hardship among families in some of the Park's more isolated hamlets.

Additional prison closures in the Adirondacks over the next couple of years—including facilities at Chateaugay, Gabriels and Mount McGregor—resulted in the loss of some five hundred jobs in a region already suffering from a poorly diversified economy that lacked the resilience needed to adjust. The region's poor economic diversification and agility, coupled with an inadequate transportation network, was further reflected in the lack of interest among potential investors in the now-vacant prisons. The closure of prison facilities in the Adirondacks illustrates what can happen with too heavy a reliance on the vagaries of state and federal budget processes and political priorities, and prisons and their supporting infrastructure are challenging to repurpose under the best of circumstances. Camp Gabriels, for example, initially had no takers, and the modern facility and twenty-seven acres that comprised the Lyon Mountain facility sold to a Canadian investor for only $140,000, the only bid submitted. According to a local elected official, "Other regions of the state not only have a better capacity to absorb the economic impact of a closure, but the real estate is also of much higher value" according to the *Adirondack Daily Enterprise* in 2013.

The story behind the closure of Camp Gabriels offers an illustration of the intersection of an overdependence on public-sector jobs, the attitudes of wealthy downstate Adirondack landowners toward the needs of local communities and citizens and community dependence on often fragile service economies. Originally built in 1897 as a sanatorium for the treatment of tuberculosis, the property comprising Camp Gabriels was sold to the state in 1982 by then owner Paul Smith's College, which had been using the site for dorms and forestry instruction. As a result of the sale, the site technically became part of the Adirondack Forest Preserve. Camp Gabriels

The former Camp Gabriels minimum security state prison. Opened in 1982, the facility was closed in 2009 and has remained vacant since. *A. Egan photo.*

was officially opened at the site as a 153-inmate minimum security facility on August 30, 1982.

But the opening of Camp Gabriels was controversial. A group calling itself Citizens Against More Prisons (CAMP) claimed that a prison would reduce the region's appeal to tourists and second-home owners. Others saw the prison as a source of reliable employment to an already economically depressed region of the Park. According to a 1981 report by Nancy Boyer-Rechlin, the St. Regis Property Owners Association, representing some forty great camps and estates on nearby Upper St. Regis and Spitfire Lakes, also opposed the establishment of Camp Gabriels. A director of the St. Regis Property Owners Association and a member of CAMP was John B. Trevor Jr.[35] In addition to his work with the St. Regis Property Owners Association to stop Camp Gabriels, Trevor also served on the Brighton Town Planning Board and attempted to introduce an amendment to the local zoning ordinance that would preclude the building of a prison on the proposed site. While Trevor's motion was not seconded, the eventual closing of Camp Gabriels by the state seemed a foregone conclusion. On January 18,

2008, local media reported that Camp Gabriels would close within a year, saving New York some $9 million per year but resulting in the loss of 136 Adirondack jobs.

As of the spring of 2020, the former Camp Gabriels remained vacant. State and local governments and other interests were trying to find a buyer for what has become something of an Adirondack white elephant while attempting to decouple the site from the forest preserve so that the land and its buildings might be sold and developed for other uses. A solution, if one exists, appears to be years away, as the state legislature considers a constitutional amendment that would allow the camp's ninety-two acres of state land to be sold or leased.

Adirondack Land Grab

The Biosphere Reserve concept has been linked to more recent efforts by the State of New York to purchase tracts of land and conservation easements to create a land bridge between core areas of the Champlain-Adirondack Biosphere Reserve, imposing further restrictions on how these new forever-wild lands might be used, especially as it relates to the use of motorized off-road vehicles and long-term timber harvesting opportunities. A 2010 survey of Northern Forest residents showed that few Adirondackers wanted the state to acquire more forest preserve land within the blue line, significantly fewer people than in any other Northern Forest state from New York to Maine.[36] Fearing the further erosion of private-sector jobs, especially in the forestry sector, in 2011, the Adirondack Park's Local Government Review Board, consisting of members appointed by the governing bodies of the twelve counties wholly or partly in the Adirondack Park, passed a resolution opposing further land purchases by the state. The land in question included some sixty thousand acres of former Finch, Pruyn and Company land in the central Adirondacks, which, at the time, was owned by the Adirondack Chapter of The Nature Conservancy (TNC). Consistent with available data, the board asserted that working forests provided more and better-paying jobs than did forests used for recreation.

In 2011, the Adirondack Council, an environmental advocacy group, accused the state-funded board of overstepping its authority, asking it to withdraw the resolution and accusing several board members of conflict of interest, citing their ties to hunting and fishing clubs on former Finch lands. The editor of the *Enterprise*, Peter Crowley, weighed in a few days later with an editorial criticizing the state for cutting funding for education while maintaining funding levels for land acquisition. The editorial went on to say that:

> *State land is wonderful, but it is a treasure we already have a great deal of—more than the depleted state Department of Environmental Conservation can adequately manage....Under recent governors, New York has rapidly bought an amazing amount of land for the Forest Preserve....The main reason the Review Board is giving in to these lobbying efforts is that forestry job losses would ensue from making these lands Forest Preserve. That's true, but it's not an entirely convincing argument. Forestry doesn't employ many people these days, and those few jobs might—this is by no means certain—be made up for economically with tourism from new Forest Preserve....A more convincing argument is that the state just can't afford to buy land right now. Those millions would be better spent easing the burden our budget crisis is placing on schools, hospitals or some other necessity.*

Nevertheless, the state of New York continued to purchase additional lands, adding to its inventory of forever-wild forests while further challenging active forest management and sustainable and meaningful rural economic development in the Park and stretching its own ability to manage those lands. In August 2012, the state reached a deal with TNC for sixty-nine thousand acres of former Finch land. This prompted further outcries about how much land is enough for the state to own, speculation about the state's endgame and concerns about the loss of jobs related to otherwise working forests. But other people, including some who had been staunchly opposed to additional state land acquisitions in the Park, were more conciliatory, conceding that there was adequate study of lands that had the greatest timber-producing potential and praising the purchase for its potential to increase access for recreation. However, criticisms directed at the state's inability to manage the lands already enrolled in the forest preserve were magnified a few months later around revelations about the lack of planning on existing state lands in the Adirondacks, primarily due to a lack of forestland management capacity within the DEC.

Criticisms of state land acquisitions in the Adirondacks are not new. In 1915, for example, the *Lake Placid News* wrote that "the proposed provision of raising arbitrarily a half-million-dollar fund annually for buying additional land for forest preserves is a dangerous scheme....Let us learn how, intelligently and economically, to govern, enjoy and conserve what forest reserves we now have before adding to our possessions of that nature and incurring the hazard of greater waste, official bungling and scandal," a criticism that has echoed for decades since. The Association for the Protection of the Adirondacks weighed in in 1980 with the following statement contained in its Seventy-Ninth Annual Report: "It has been the position of this Association that the existing proportions of 40% state–60% private were a good balance and that except for certain key tracts, additional open space is best protected by the acquisition of development or conservation easements. The fact is, however, that the state continues to acquire lands as they become available or development threatens," while the DEC continued to struggle to manage existing forest preserve. Suggesting that initiatives to add acreage to the forest preserve could backfire on those who were more staunchly preservationist, the association continued to argue that "as the state adds to its holdings, the timber industry and labor pressures to amend Article XIV to allow lumbering on parts of the Forest Preserve will, in the long run, become overwhelming."

There was also local opposition to Governor Mario Cuomo's August 2012 decision for the state to purchase the former Finch lands from The Nature Conservancy, including criticism from the Fulton County Board of Supervisors, which claimed that the purchase would harm local economies in the Park, estimating a loss of three hundred forestry-sector jobs. One local official claimed that the land, once sold to the state, "will never be logged again. It's just one more nail in the coffin of any kind of economic engine in the Adirondacks," according to a report in the *Adirondack Daily Enterprise* on October 17 of that year. A member of the Adirondack Park Local Government Review Board referred to the sale as "very disappointing for local government and residents and anyone who depends on the forest industry for their livelihood….It's very sad for residents and workers in the Adirondacks," the *Enterprise* reported. This led the newspaper to call for a more clearly defined endgame regarding state land purchases in the Adirondacks. "The state has not said when it might stop growing the Preserve," observed the editor of the *Enterprise* in 2012. The editorial went on to cite the 1987 Adirondack Park State Land Master Plan, Acquisition Policy Recommendation No. 11, which states that "due to the importance of the forest products industry to the economy of the Adirondack region, bulk acreage purchases in fee should not normally be made where highly productive forest land is involved." As stated by a procurement forester from International Paper Company, forestland purchases by the state have

Top: Oval Wood Dish, Tupper Lake, circa 1930. Beginning in 1918, the hardwood manufacturer of renewable, recyclable and compostable wood products was an anchor for Tupper Lake's forest-based economy, at one time employing over five hundred year-round workers. OWD closed in 1964. *Goff-Nelson Memorial Library*.

Bottom: International Paper mill in Piercefield. Once reliant on the paper industry for year-round employment, after the closing of the International Paper mill in 1933 Piercefield's population dropped precipitously, from 1,330 residents in 1930 to 667 in 1940. *Goff-Nelson Memorial Library*.

"caused us to have to go further away to get the same volume of wood. Whenever land gets purchased by the state and put into the forest preserve, it means that you can't touch it. So even though we're the only mill that's located within the park and we have a world of timber around the mill, most of it you can't touch," according to an NCPR report titled "Do Big Adirondack Conservation Deals Hurt Loggers?" on October 1 of that year. Putting it more bluntly, a local Adirondack businessman claimed that these land purchases by the state have "killed the logging industry" in the Park, reported the *Enterprise*.

Referring to the Adirondack Park's Local Government Review Board, the *Adirondack Daily Enterprise* reported in 2011, "One of the main arguments put forth by the local government resolution against the purchase of Forest Reserve is that working forests provide more jobs than those used for recreation." Data appear to support this contention. A study conducted by New York's Department of Environmental Conservation reported that, statewide, forest-based manufacturing contributed $6.9 billion in value of shipments in 2005, while forest-based recreation generated $1.9 billion, suggesting strong potential in the heavily forested six-million-acre Adirondack Park for the development of a more viable forest products industry.[37] In addition, the same report claimed that forestry and logging provided 57,202 jobs and a payroll of over $2.1 billion in the state as a whole, while forest-related recreation brought 14,600 jobs and a payroll of $300 million, reflecting average salaries of $36,712 and $20,548 for forest products and forest recreation employment, respectively, and supporting studies that describe the low wages and seasonal employment associated with jobs in forest recreation. Importantly, the study states that every one thousand acres of forest land in New York supports 3.0 forest-based manufacturing, forestry and logging jobs and 0.8 forest-related tourism and recreation jobs, countering assertions made by TNC and others about the value to Adirondack communities of a primarily recreation-based economy.

So, where did all the Adirondack loggers go? A University of Maine study of Adirondack loggers and logging business owners suggested that among the reasons for a decline in the region's logging capacity were uncertainties about forestland ownership in the Park, an opinion not reported by logging business owners in the other three northern forest states of Vermont, New Hampshire and Maine.[38] Over 90 percent of logging business owners in the Adirondack region indicated that this uncertainty was an important or very important barrier to maintaining their businesses, while this was true of only 61 percent of those logging businesses located outside the Park. Adirondack loggers were also significantly older than their Northern Forest counterparts, further calling into question the future of the forestry sector in the Park.

Nevertheless, the New York Department of Environmental Conservation defended the sale of these lands to the state by citing a study that placed the most productive working forests in conservation easements rather than sold in fee as state preserve lands. According to reporting by Chris Knight of the *Enterprise* in 2010, an official from TNC—described by Brian Mann of NCPR in 2017 as an environmental organization that serves as "a land and power broker, helping state agencies figure out how to preserve massive tracts of Park land worth hundreds of millions of dollars…[and] playing midwife on projects that redefined wilderness areas and opened vast new landscapes for hiking and paddling"—responded to criticisms of the former Finch land sales and easements by saying that "purchase of the conservation easements will help support the regional economy. This is a $30 million investment in the Adirondack economy. The deal will keep the

The lumberjack statue in the working-class town of Tupper Lake. The town was once the timber capital of the Adirondacks, but according to the 2000 census, over one-third of its population lived below the poverty line. *A. Egan photo.*

forest products industry in the Adirondacks competitive and viable.... This easement allows for continued sustainable forestry and helps protect jobs at the mill and related suppliers. That's a significant number of positions in this challenged economy in the state."

Somewhat at odds with these statements, however, about a year later, the same TNC spokesperson stated that "in the Adirondacks, recreation is a bigger part of the economy than logging; the forest economy is a very very small percentage of the Adirondack economy [and the] recreation tourism economy is a much larger percentage," according to Mike Lynch of the *Enterprise* in 2011. His argument appeared to ignore that the expansion of the Adirondack forever-wild forest preserve and regulations on private forests that are unique to the Park had already constrained forest industry there, likely leading to a contraction of that industry relative to recreation and tourism within the blue line. In addition, data reported in 2010 by Graham Cox and others suggested that tourism too often provided low-wage seasonal employment. According to a 2014 report by Brian Mann, "many tourism positions are poorly paid, part time and/or seasonal, offering few benefits...average weekly wages of $255...with many of the jobs going to low-skilled workers and youth, especially in the summer," the region's peak tourist season.

Of course, second-home owners and tourists have been and continue to be important residents and consumers of Adirondack goods and services. But data suggest serious flaws in the notion that an economy centered on outdoor recreation and tourism can take the place of a more diversified economy that includes manufacturing. A 2014 tourism study for Essex County found that 85 percent of the visitors to the Adirondacks did so for hiking. Winter sports drew far fewer visits, despite Essex County being a center for winter-related outdoor activity, such as skiing and venues for winter Olympic sports. As a result, visitations are highly seasonal, with July and August the most popular period—consistent with the high demand for short-duration hiking-related activity—and far fewer visits in the winter months. And the regional economy's reliance on an event calendar highlighted by the occasional canoe race contested by hardened locals and hockey camps for more privileged downstate kids brings only localized, short-term economic relief from an otherwise bleak Adirondack reality of expanding pockets of unemployment and poverty, declining year-round populations and struggling school systems.

PART III

MODEL FOR THE WORLD

The Adirondack Park is a success story that provides context for the Park and its working forest.
—John Collins, former chair of the Adirondack Park Agency, 1994

Cars were parked illegally up and down the Adirondack Loj Road. Waste of all kinds piled up on the trails. Labor Day weekend brought more people to the Adirondack High Peaks than ever before. The situation was dangerous for drivers, hikers and wildlife.
—Goren et al., "Summits Overrun over Labor Day," 2016.

5
AN ADIRONDACK FUTURE

The problem is that "everybody's property is nobody's property" so that no one will conserve the natural resource. Individuals pursuing their own interests lead to overuse of the natural resource and perhaps to its destruction.
—Vrooman, 1975, writing about the Adirondack Park

Given its quirky past and sometimes dysfunctional present, it remains curious that many support the notion that the Adirondacks could serve as a land-use model for the world while at the same time acknowledging massive inputs of energy into the Park from beyond the blue line, a declining and aging population and jobless rates that are among the highest in state. Despite these harsh realities, a former chair of the Adirondack Park Agency wrote that the Park "works," remaining "a vast area of private working forest, public preserve lands, and communities that have fared reasonably well economically in a period of overall decline in the Northeast (but with pockets of chronic and unacceptable poverty)."[39] The author's parenthetical reference to persistent poverty in the Adirondacks is a reminder of the sometimes cynical nature of Park politics, "chronic and unacceptable poverty" reduced to a collateral, parenthetical afterthought. Given the region's past and its current realities, there are some future Adirondack conditions that appear reasonably certain, outcomes of the evolution of rich man's paradise.

Fewer, Older, Poorer

As we've seen, according to a 2009 report for the New York State Department of Labor, the population of the Park is in decline, and those who are left behind represent an aging cohort of year-round locals with limited prospects. Numerous studies have painted a bleak picture of the region's economic and demographic realities, and the impacts of a rich man's paradise on locals and local economies will continue to be far-reaching. Housing availability and its impact on community stability is one example. In 1989, Cornell's Adirondack Household Research Project concluded that "lot-size requirements and other APA regulation to protect the environment have driven housing costs up to a point where many people trying to purchase a primary home in the area can't afford it, creating a housing crisis. Secondary home purchases are not being affected to the same extent....Most people up here that I have talked to do want to protect the Adirondacks, but they want job opportunities, too," reported the *Glens Falls Post-Star* in July of that year. The situation has not improved.

According to a 2014 *Albany Times Union* article titled "Graying of Adirondacks Presents Future Challenges," a report covering 103 towns and villages and sources that included the Program for Applied Demographics at Cornell University, the Department of Environmental Conservation, the Department of Education and several other state agencies: "While older people do bring money and experience, they are often retired and not worried about finding work, something that is critical in attracting young people who will create growing families. By 2030, more than a third of the Park residents will be 60 or older. And when those people begin to die, it is not clear who will come in to replace them, which could lead to further depopulation in the Adirondacks." A Park with fewer children will result in further struggles for many of its school districts, resulting in school closures and consolidations. That there will be fewer young people will also challenge volunteer fire and ambulance services, forcing a transition to more and better-paid emergency staff to avoid increased response times. This will drive up taxes, "which would further discourage young families from moving in but would be less of a deterrent to more affluent retirees." Reversing these trends will require more year-round jobs, according to one opinion leader, "and jobs cannot only be in tourism, which sometimes do not pay well, but also in some sort of revived manufacturing....We have to ask ourselves whether our

Declining populations resulted in the closing of Holy Name Catholic Church in Tupper Lake in 2019. *A. Egan photo.*

communities can survive without a supermarket, without a gas station, without a school," realities to which some Adirondack hamlets have already been forced to adjust.

Apart from the stark demographic realities of a declining and aging population, among the contexts for an Adirondack future are struggling local communities and a poorly diversified regional economy suffering from years of neglect. Highlighting the two 2017 graduates of Long Lake Central School, "Of the ten smallest school districts in upstate New York, seven are tucked away in the Adirondacks. And they are tiny....Why not merge? [Putnam Central School Superintendent] Bouchard said this option has been considered, but it was discovered that local people's taxes would increase if they did." According to the superintendent of Long Lake, "The most critical component for all rural school districts in the Adirondacks is bringing young people to the area to live year-round, and to do that we need to increase and diversify employment opportunities," as reported in the *Enterprise* in August of that year. But, according to a Northern Forest Center report, among the factors that young people consider when determining where to live are broadband access, jobs that can lead to careers, vibrant downtowns and arts and entertainment. Much of the Adirondack region lacks these basic attributes.

The notion of rural community stability and local economic diversification, however, has collided with the conversion of private lands to forest preserve within the blue line, often playing out as tension between year-round Adirondack residents and environmental interests from inside and outside the Park. One example of the drive to acquire more land to add to the Park's forest preserve, irrespective of the negative impacts on local economies and the state's inability to adequately manage the Park's existing forever-wild lands, was the push for the state to purchase the thirty-six-thousand-acre Whitney Park, put on the market in 2020 for $180 million. Environmental groups and private citizens lobbied to have the state buy the property, which includes more than twenty lakes and ponds. The Town of Long Lake, however, opposed converting the site from private ownership to forest preserve, citing the further erosion of local employment, including jobs related to the stewardship of the property's forests and the maintenance of its roads, houses and other buildings. Long Lake's population had been steadily declining since 1910, when there were over a thousand residents. At the 2010 census, the town's population was 711, over 15 percent of whom were living below the poverty line. Nevertheless, even during a pandemic that stretched the state's coffers and threatened the livelihoods of some local residents, and ignoring the town's challenging demographic and economic realities, some continued to push for the state to make the purchase a high priority.

An editorial in the *Lake Placid News* on August 13, 2020, titled "State Should Not Buy Whitney Park," presented additional arguments in opposition to the state adding the estate to the Adirondack Park's forest preserve. The editor asserted that local Adirondack communities have realized few, if any, economic benefits from the designation of the 18,400-acre St. Regis Canoe Area. The more recent inclusion of the Boreas Ponds Tract to the Park's forest preserve has, so far, not brought an economic boost to the Newcomb area, the editor argued. Other reasons for not purchasing the estate and designating it as part of the forest preserve included the already strapped Department of Environmental Conservation, which is charged with managing the state's forest preserve, and the overuse of the Park's forest preserve "when there are just too many people on the trails," converting more private lands to preserve "doing more damage than protection." The editorial was subsequently the target of forest preserve advocates, who did not address the possible impacts of the state acquiring the property on local employment and community stability. Instead, they viewed the opportunity of including the estate in the Adirondacks' forest preserve relative to their own outdoor recreation interests, reminiscent of the trail of ambivalence toward local families and communities shown by others throughout the Park's history.

The Adirondack region will continue to contend with the persistent patterns of seasonal unemployment characteristic of a regional economy that is poorly diversified and heavily dependent on outdoor recreation, seasonal second-home owners and a weakened manufacturing sector.[40] Confirming what is already known to struggling local Adirondackers, one observer of the Adirondack Park experience suggested that most of the growth in employment in the region has been in lower-wage service and trade industries, at the expense of significant losses in higher-wage construction and manufacturing jobs, and that due to the area's dependence on tourism and outdoor recreation, sharp seasonal swings in unemployment have been commonplace.[41]

But what of the visitors to the Adirondacks, the tourists and recreationists who support one of the region's most important economic sectors, albeit one that is low-paying and seasonal?

More Crowded…

At least with tourists, as the year-round population continues to decline, longtime Adirondack residents unable to find meaningful employment in the Park's seasonal, low-paying recreation-dominated economy. According to some critics of the twenty-first-century Adirondack outdoor experience, so-called peak-baggers will continue to throng to popular, already well-worn and eroded wilderness hiking trails. On November 13, 2008, the *Lake Placid News* reported, "For two or three hours almost every afternoon, cars can be seen parked along state Route 73 while their occupants scan the forests for moose."

Despite the broader, Park-wide economic benefits of Adirondack tourism—outside of the tourist towns of Lake George, Lake Placid and Old Forge—more remote Adirondack communities have often been left behind. Once reliant on resource extraction and manufacturing, followed by mostly defunct prison economies, tourism has not filled the void in these depressed, off-the-beaten-path communities. To those who believe that increasing tourism to the region simply requires more and better marketing, one local expert wrote, as reported by the *Adirondack Almanac* in 2012: "The bottom line: we can market the heck out of Childwold, N.Y. as a destination, but the visitors will stay in Lake Placid anyway." Not unlike Murray and his followers some 150 years ago, data suggest that most of today's Adirondack tourists are less interested in a backcountry experience than in more accommodating tourist towns such as Lake George and Lake Placid, with an occasional one-hour hike on crowded nearby forest trails thrown in. Again, the tourism marketing expert: "In August, 2012, the 'Outdoors' pages on lakeplacid.com received over 50,000-page views, and the hiking-specific pages received over 12,500 views. But the breakdown is interesting: The website offers categories of hikes as follows: one to two hour, two to four hour, four-hour, over eight-hour hikes and the forty-six high peaks. Which of those categories is most popular? The most page views, at about 4,800, were on the 1-2 hour hike pages. The least, at just under 400, were those over 8 hours. The longer the hike, the fewer the page views." The author's conclusion? "And so, according to our statistics, most visitors plan to hike up a short trail such as Mount Jo or Baxter Mountain, and then return to the closest resort setting for a beer. And that resort is likely Lake Placid."

Although many visitors to the Adirondacks embrace and respect the Park and its wilderness character, one study found that recreationists in the Adirondacks, specifically hikers in the High Peaks, "are more sensitive to crowding than environmental impacts" such as soil compaction and erosion on and proximate to hiking trails,[42] raising serious questions about the compatibility of outdoor recreation and environmental stewardship similar to those that might have been raised in the mid-nineteenth to early twentieth centuries when throngs of Murray's Fools were responsible for overcrowding hiking trails, unethical exploitation of fish and game and carelessness with fire that compromised many Adirondack ecosystems. According to a former New York State Department of Environmental Conservation commissioner, "We've come to the tipping point where it's necessary to make some changes in how we administer the Park. One of the big considerations is how to raise revenue to do that," suggesting that a fee system "would be one way to get some resources to the department" while also managing tourist numbers and resulting environmental impacts.

An article in the *Adirondack Explorer* in 2017 titled "Controlling Crowds in the High Peaks" painted this bleak picture: "Parking lots have overflowed along Route 73, summits have become packed on holiday weekends, trails have seen more erosion, the number of search and rescues has risen, and litter and human waste has accumulated in high-congestion areas." Despite the efforts of the Department of Environmental Conservation to manage these challenges and reduce footfall in the Adirondack wilderness, a 2018 study by the Adirondack Council reported in the *Enterprise* found that thirty-five Adirondack trailhead parking areas with a combined capacity of 1,000 cars had more than 2,100 cars during peak weekends in the fall of 2017. The 73-car-capacity trailhead parking area for the hike to popular Cascade Mountain averaged 240 cars on weekends, while the 10-car-capacity area at the trailhead for Ampersand Mountain had 64 cars. While the focus of the article was on traffic and pedestrian safety associated with the overflow, the article also mentioned the environmental damage to trails and mountain ecosystems resulting from overuse of Adirondack trails, as well as the accumulation of human waste and trash near trailheads and along hiking trails. A couple of weeks later, an editorial in the *Adirondack Daily Enterprise* continued to decry the damage already being done to Adirondack ecosystems by some recreationists, describing "the garbage, the graffiti and the gardens of toilet paper and feces from people who use the woods as a toilet," suggesting that the "DEC doesn't really have an effective way of dealing with all this" and asking the rhetorical question: "Is list-based peak-bagging worth it?"

Commenting on the crowding and increasing lack of experience and wilderness ethics among many Adirondack hikers, and reminding us of Murray's Fools, in 2017, the *Albany Times Union* reported the following:

> *Throngs of visitors have also affected the condition of the state's public lands and the environment in the peaks and trails. Popular summits like Mount Marcy and Cascades are often overrun with hikers. Human waste has been left in footpaths and alpine flora and vegetation has been trampled, said Neil Woodworth, executive director of the Adirondack Mountain Club. Between seven and 10 million people visit the Adirondacks every year.... "The people visiting have changed over the past few years," he said. "They're less experienced and frequently don't have a family history.... Climbing mountains has become a popular social experience," Woodworth said. "People want to advertise their feats on social media."*

According to a frustrated local town official speaking to the *Enterprise* in 2019, "it's just been the wild west" on the hiking trails of the High Peaks region. Or, as Adirondack Harry wrote about Gilded Age visitors to the Adirondacks over

This page: Overcrowded trailhead parking in the Adirondacks on the July 4, 2020 weekend. One study found that hikers in the High Peaks were more concerned about crowding on trails than their own environmental impacts, raising questions about the wilderness ethics of some visitors and the health of some Adirondack ecosystems. *Both from A. Egan photos.*

one hundred years earlier, "The carries and trails were thronged." But the problem appeared only to worsen the following year, as tourists, cooped up at home by the pandemic, decided to de-isolate and visit the Adirondacks in record numbers. Solutions to illegal parking and overcrowded mountain trails and peaks, however, remained elusive. During the summer of 2020, the *Lake Placid News* printed an editorial in opposition to a permit system for trails in the High Peaks, suggesting instead that the state invest more in hiring forest rangers to patrol the Park's backcountry. Makes sense. This is the job that most DEC rangers had signed up for and were trained to do. However, in addition to the politics of permitting—Who gets permits and who doesn't? Should year-round Adirondackers or New York State residents receive preferential treatment? How would the process be managed from beginning to end?—a permit system would appear to add another layer of coordination and enforcement to a situation that saw historically high hiker footfall in 2020, as well as some 150 more rescues than the average number of rescues over the previous five years, according to an APA spokesperson.

At the same time, however, the *Lake Placid News* editor also recommended providing "ample parking for the crowds," which, while alleviating roadside congestion, would appear to only exacerbate the problem of too much footfall on already overworked hiking trails, further stressing trailside and mountaintop ecosystems. About two weeks later, parking records were broken at one popular High Peaks trailhead; a hiker's campfire turned into a forest fire that took several days to manage; a jeep bypassed 2.6 miles of hiking trails by driving on a posted, abandoned logging road on forest preserve land; and graffiti was discovered on rocks and trees on one mountain. For many tourists, fines for such transgressions are now simply considered part of the cost of a hiking trip to the Adirondacks. "Parking fines are not working as a deterrent," according to one APA employee. Fines are low enough so that "they are just factored into the cost of the hike....(Parking) fines just don't match the infractions." One solution offered by a Park official was simply to limit parking, especially along roads, and have the towns tow offending vehicles, relieving the DEC of having to play meter maid to a recalcitrant tourist public.

Still, the calls to expand parking areas to account for vehicular spillover onto nearby thoroughfares, further jamming roads and trails, continued. Others, opposed to the issuance of permits to manage and limit "wilderness" users, have suggested that more education was the answer but did not offer how educating tourists gets at the basic problem of overuse, too many people, too much footfall. And what is the educational message for those who park and camp under signs that explicitly prohibit those activities? How about for delinquent graffiti artists and disoriented jeep drivers? Do their actions suffer from a lack of information, some might reasonably ask?

Wilderness over-tourism is no longer simply a challenge for the Adirondacks' High Peaks region. As more and more tourists eschew that charismatic but now overcrowded region of the Park for more outlying destinations, other Adirondack places are experiencing the impacts of human spillage. On a July weekend during the 2020 pandemic, the outdoors columnist for the *Adirondack Daily Enterprise* found a packed trailhead parking lot and observed heavy and careless use of trails into the Seward Range, typically a relatively quiet destination. Contending that limiting parking may not be a reliable method of crowd control—determined hikers simply park illegally—and arriving at a fair permitting system nearly impossible, the columnist soon found tents pitched beneath signs that read "Camping Prohibited" and campsites that were being established next to a brook and alongside the trail. More recently, parking problems near the trailhead of the popular but relatively small peak Mount Baker, one of the Saranac Lake area's 6er peaks (a way of increasing tourism in the sometimes overlooked Saranac Lake region, if you bag all six summits and you're officially "a 6er"), were the subject of some acrimony. Even Donaldson understood what was beginning to happen to the Park. The Adirondacks have been changed from "a great wild spot with a few parks, into a great park with a few wild spots," he seemed to lament, although, given his background, he was likely more interested in preserving a wilderness playground for the wealthy than in preserving mountain and aquatic ecosystems. That was a hundred years ago.

But there are challenges to Adirondack tourism that are unrelated to the unethical backcountry behavior of some of the Park's visitors. Apparently referring to a more casual appearance of the Adirondacks contrasted with an often-gentrified, bucolic look of the Vermont landscape, one observer described "Vermont [as looking] like Austria, while this side of Lake Champlain is more like Bulgaria."[43] And some tourists—the primary supporters of an Adirondack service economy—appear to agree. Although strictly anecdotal, travel forums comparing Vermont with the Adirondacks consistently describe the Green Mountain State as charming, diverse and progressive, with a stable, entrepreneurial economy. The "Adies," on the other hand, are more often described as depressed and unkempt, with boarded-up downtowns. While some proud and independent Adirondackers might just as soon have it that way, this aesthetic disparity is, in part, a symptom of a poorly diversified economy in a place that is subject to regulations and constraints not found outside its blue line.

More Wildfire Habitat

Research around the nature of past and future climate change and its impacts on the Adirondack region has been a bit unsettled. Some have predicted an increase in frontal and gusty wind events related to elevated temperatures in the Adirondacks, leading to speculation on the impacts of wind on recreation, such as canoeing, and wildlife and plant growth.[44] Other recreational impacts are a shortened winter recreation season and toxic algal blooms that compromise drinking-water supplies and discourage summer lake recreation.[45] If these predictions come to pass, such inconveniences to recreationists may be the least of the Park's worries.

Irrespective of the often-conflicting science on local and regional manifestations and impacts of a changing climate, current consensus is that, as with much of North America, the future climate of the Adirondacks, while understandably couched in uncertainty, is likely to be warmer, with more extreme weather events. Local ecologists have predicted that Adirondack forests will experience increased stress, making them more susceptible to diseases, likely leading to a significant increase in the amount of dead and dried forest fuel, especially in the Park's unmanaged forest preserve lands. Such a scenario will result in even more windthrown forest fuel accumulations from increasingly severe weather events. In addition, according to the seminal report, "Responding to Climate Change in New York State," there may be a greater frequency, duration and intensity of summer droughts, although winter precipitation is expected to increase.[46] If the summer drought prediction holds, then this and the accumulation of woody fuels in the Park's forever-wild forests, where potentially hazardous woody fuels are not managed, reduced or removed, suggest heightened risk for severe spring and summer wildfires in the Adirondacks, similar to what the region experienced in the late 1800s and early 1900s—fires that clearly demonstrated that, under the right conditions of prolonged drought and heat, Adirondack forests can burn catastrophically.

Unmanaged Adirondack Forest Preserve not only makes the forest resource less responsive to future forest products markets but also results in forests that are less resilient in response to changes in climate. In addition, if recreational use of these lands continues at its present rate, this will increase the potential for careless human-caused forest-fire ignitions—a major source of forest fires going back to the nineteenth and early twentieth centuries and the invasion of Murray's Fools. Given the contraction of the forestry sector in the Adirondacks, it will be a tragic irony if future catastrophic wildfires

This page: Forest-fire fuels accumulating in the Adirondack Park's forest preserve. While woody fuels are also present in the Park's private forests, regulations prevent the reduction or removal of ground and ladder fuels on the Park's forever-wild public lands, increasing the risk of major forest fires in the region. Top: *A. Egan photo*; bottom: *W. Egan photo*.

Part of a mural in the Adirondack town of Warrensburgh, painted by E. Cockcroft in 1976, illustrating the importance of industry to early Adirondack communities. *A. Egan photo.*

in the Park will be blamed on a lack of forest management rather than on the historical scapegoat of too much forest management. Just over a century ago, the 1914 Fourth Annual Report of the Conservation Commission agreed, suggesting of the Park's forever-wild policy that "the time has come, however, when modifications of this drastic policy may be safely considered. We now know—the scientific forester of our time tells us—what was not appreciated twenty years ago, that selective cutting and removal of ripe timber is beneficial to the forests, apart from lessening the fire danger.… We therefore reaffirm our support for the constitutional amendment by the Legislature of 1913, which would permit the removal of ripe timber."

Supporting the notion of an unhealthy buildup of forest fuels, in 2013, NCPR's Mann reported on the development of an Adirondack "junk forest" on the Park's forestlands that "threatens the long-term environmental health of the Adirondacks, as well as the health of the North Country's logging industry," such as it is. Unfortunately, unless one assumes government subsidy for the reduction of hazardous fuels, the lack of primary and secondary forest-products processing in the Park, combined with a decline in the region's logging sector, will likely conspire to severely challenge the efficacy and cohesion of region-wide fuel reduction efforts.[47]

History tells us that, under the right conditions of fuel loads and natural or human-caused ignition, the Adirondacks will experience severe wildfire. Forest fires have occurred naturally in the Adirondacks, and, while not as common as other causes, such as campfires, lightning remains a wildfire ignition source. Records indicate an overall increase in the frequency of Adirondack fires caused by lightning over a brief span in the early 1900s: 1908, nine fires; 1909, eight; 1910, eleven; 1911, sixty-five. About a half century later, lightning was reported to have caused at least eight forest fires in the Adirondacks over a period of just a few days during an exceptionally dry spell in the summer of 1964. Some twenty years later, during the dry summer of 1983, the dozens of fires that had been reported in late July and early August, most were caused by lightning, according to a report in the *Plattsburgh Press Republican* that year.

Early state conservationists recognized the dangers associated with the collision between fire suppression and forever-wild forested landscapes but knew little or nothing about a warming climate. Nevertheless, the Association for the Protection of the Adirondacks recognized as early as 1915 the need to reduce forest fuels, stating, "The power to remove dead timber, but not to sell it, and to construct fire trails, the association believes, will conduce to the safety of the forests and is a step in the right direction," according to the *Lake Placid News*. Earlier that year, the *Lake Placid News* stated: "The land of the state should be unlocked so that the forest floor may be safely and sanely

According to state reports, recreationists, farmers and, later, locomotives were responsible for most of the fires in the Adirondacks. A Hunting Party in the Woods, *1856, Frederic Rondel.*

This page: The scenic beauty of the Adirondack Park can mask ecological challenges like invasive species, hiker-worn and eroded forest trails and the accumulation of forest-fire fuels, as well as social realities, such as rural poverty and a history of exclusion. *Top*: *W. Egan*; *bottom*: *A. Egan photos*.

cleared of inflammable deadwood and underbrush." Yet instead of heeding these admonitions, Adirondack politics has chosen instead to continue to engage in a polemic around interpretations of the forever-wild clause in the state's constitution, predisposing the Adirondacks and the region to an increasing likelihood of major wildfire.

Warming temperatures also suggest an increase in forest insects and diseases and their destructive activity, including some forest pests that have never before been seen in Adirondack forests, resulting in current and future forests that are less resilient and more susceptible to disease. The hemlock wooly adelgid has already begun to have an impact on the region's hemlock forests, while the emerald ash borer has also found its way into the Park, decimating ash trees as it moves north. Both invasions are due in part, we are told, to rising Adirondack temperatures. An absence of active forest management on public lands in the Park, including forest sanitation harvesting, will encourage the spread of forest disease and pests and further contribute to an accumulation of hazardous fuels to feed Adirondack wildfires. Of course, wildfires and insect and disease outbreaks do not respect landownership boundaries. While the Adirondack forest preserve lands could be a source of hazardous fuels, forest disease inoculum and insect pests, the impacts of this will be felt not only on lands designated as forever wild but also on all forestlands in the Park and in the region.

6

IN THE END

When you live in the Adirondacks, you don't have far to fall.
—A local Adirondack resident when asked by the author in 2009 how the financial crisis was impacting him and his family

Despite its natural beauty, data suggest that today's Adirondack Park is wobbling precariously on all elements of the three-legged stool that support the concept of sustainability: environment, economy and society. The roots of the problem are connected to several strands: the canonization of Adirondack icons who do not hold up under scrutiny but are repeatedly exhumed and often misrepresented when support for a Park requires heroes to whom to tether a preservationist ideal, ambivalent about the region's working class; questionable backcountry ethics practiced by the very people who advocated for a forever-wild park; often fabulized threads of Adirondack history that have misinformed and persisted into the twenty-first century; a confounding of the terms *forest preserve* and *forest reserve* to the detriment of ecosystem health and working-class economies; a vilification of manufacturing, particularly in the forestry sector, in favor of a seasonal, low-wage caretaker economy; and surreptitious attempts to deliver the region to some form of public land-management authority—a biosphere reserve, a northern forest, a national park.

Concerns about the creation of an Adirondack rich man's paradise, to be enjoyed by wealthy dilettantes and "sports," have echoed repeatedly since the nineteenth century. Yet, clearly, despite its checkered history, there are many Adirondack visitors and seasonal second-home owners who appreciate the ecological, economic and social values and challenges extant in the notion of a park and who bring much-needed opportunity, perspectives and diversity to the community. In a recurring, often distracting and generally unproductive climate of polemicized argumentation about managing agencies, land-use regulations, environmental advocacy, local economies and community sustainability, this cannot be overemphasized. However, the question of *how all interests can work together in a more mutualistic relationship that values the synergies between community and ecology* appears only rarely to have been seriously and consistently considered. In such a place, people can consider themselves environmentalists and still advocate for sustainable economic development; local year-round residents can be vocal about their sense of marginalization but also recognize the value of visitors and second-home owners as seasonal friends and neighbors; and all may formatively express disagreement about Adirondack bureaucracies and politics, without resorting to increased polarization. A place where we allow an Adirondack future to be informed by a sometimes-disjointed Adirondack past, but not necessarily defined by it.

Reaching back one last time to 1885 and the First Annual Report of the Forest Commission of the State of New York, there was this warning: "It is *not* the object of forestry, at least in this country, to maintain the woodlands as

This page and opposite: Poverty's midden. "There is nothing Appalachian about rural poverty in northern New York," according to one observer of the Adirondack experience. All: *A. Egan photos*.

a shelter for game and as a region of pleasure resort to those who can afford the time and means for this kind of enjoyment" (p. 66; emphasis in original). Indeed, what is occurring on the Park's forest preserve lands has little to do with forestry—science-informed practices that reflect resource stewardship, ecosystem health, forest and community sustainability and, in its most highly evolved realization, an emphasis on social justice and democratic processes, especially as they relate to publicly owned forestlands.

Can the Park have it all? Can it be a place that preserves certain landscape values, while also maintaining human communities with sustainable economies and ecosystems that thrive in harmony with those values—all in the context of a rich man's paradise? Today, outcomes of the Adirondack region's long history of power and politics include: low-paying, seasonal employment and underemployment; an exodus of working-class year-round residents; persistence of a Murray's Fools phenomenon that benefits a couple of gentrified Adirondack places; natural ecosystems at risk of being compromised by human excesses and carelessness; and a lack of local and regional economic resilience and diversification. Describing Adirondackers, one observer wrote, "They're a dying breed; there are only a few families left in our town. I recently asked one of them what his attitude about life was, and he said, "I more or less live day to day and try to figure out how to get the things I want without going into debt or asking anybody for anything,"[48] leaving us to wonder whether to interpret his attitude as one of staunch independence or dispirited resignation.

Aspects of today's Adirondacks are reminiscent of the characters to whom much of its unsettled and jumbled history has been curiously connected and its present-day political polemics rationalized: of the inconsistently competent Colvin—careless, erratic, hypocritical; of the backcountry bragger, Adirondack Murray—misleading, contradictory, self-infatuated; and of the other "Adirondack," the romanticist, four-flusher Radford—idealistic, naive, privileged. By continuing to accept a revisionist narrative that serves special interests—of biosphere reserves, national parks, northern forests—but rarely the interests of Park communities and ecosystems, we both inherit and perpetuate a place where characters of questionable values and motivations are considered icons and, the historical record suggests, the wealthy and politically influential are allowed to create their sense of wilderness at the expense of a withering working class, dwindling local communities and an increasingly threatened natural environment.

That's neither a model for the world nor a blueprint for quality of life and sustainable natural ecosystems and human communities inside a blue line.

NOTES

Chapter 1

1. H. Radford, *Adirondack Murray, a Biographical Appreciation* (New York: Broadway Publishing Company, 1905).
2. W.H.H. Murray, *Adventures in the Wilderness* (Boston: Cupples and Heard, 1869).
3. Joel Tyler Headley, later to become secretary of state of New York, was a member of the American Party, described as a far-right political movement that was anti-Catholic, nativist, anti-immigration and xenophobic. He wrote two books about the Adirondack region: *The Adirondack; or, Life in the Woods* (New York: Charles Scribner, 1849) and *Letters from the Backwoods and the Adirondac* (New York: John S. Taylor, 1850).
4. W.C. White, *Adirondack Country* (Syracuse, NY: Syracuse University Press, 1954).
5. William F. Martin was a confidant of Abraham Lincoln and owner of a grand hotel on Lower Saranac Lake where Murray and other notables from political and corporate high society would stay when visiting the Adirondacks. The hotel featured billiards, bowling alleys and a croquet lawn.

Chapter 2

6. Headley, *The Adirondack; or, Life in the Woods*. In this passage, when he mentions "driving trees," Headley is not referring to river driving, but to a technique that is today commonly called "domino felling." Domino felling is described by the Occupational Safety and Health Administration's logging standard as "the partial cutting of multiple trees which are left standing and then pushed over with

a pusher tree," a widely practiced, often efficient but very dangerous directional felling method.

7. Hammond, *Wild Northern Scenes*.
8. Beyond his general ambivalence toward Adirondack "natives" (i.e., local Adirondackers), and especially the region's logging community, Donaldson wrote with apparent disparagement about others who were not like him. Describing an African American community near Lake Placid, Donaldson wrote, "The last touch of pure negroism was a large but dilapidated red flag that floated above the settlement, bearing the half-humorous, half-pathetic legend 'Timbuctoo'—a name that was applied to the whole vicinity for several years" (Donaldson, *A History of the Adirondacks*, 6). In fairness to Donaldson, he also refers to abolitionism as a "righteous cause" and to those escaping from slavery as "poor hunted fugitives." Readers are encouraged to consider Donaldson's chapter "John Brown of North Elba," found at the beginning of his book's second volume, in order to appreciate the full context.
9. Erickson, "In Search of Sustainable Development: Lessons in Application from the Adirondack Park."
10. Young, *Special Report on Immigration*.
11. Eben Tourjee was a conductor, musician and educator who helped to establish the New England Conservatory of Music. He was awarded an honorary doctorate from Wesleyan University in 1869, thus the reference to him as Dr. Tourjee.
12. William Dodge was a well-known and respected "state game protector" during this period.
13. Wynn, "Deplorably Dark and Demoralized Lumberers,."
14. P. Welsh, *Jacks, Jobbers and Kings: Logging in the Adirondacks, 1850–1950* (Utica, NY: North Country Books, 1995).
15. The State of New York, *Third Annual Report of the Conservation Commission, 1913* (Albany, NY: 1914) cited the carelessness of forest users, especially smokers and fishermen, for "the wicked destruction of the 'people's playground'" (p. 22). The same report called for the "utilization of ripe timber" on the forest preserve (p. 24). Again, loggers and logging activity were not implicated in any fires during the unusually droughty and disastrous 1913 fire year.

Chapter 3

16. Halper, "'A Rich Man's Paradise'."
17. Thomson, *An Address before the Albany Institute on the Adirondack Wilderness*.
18. Burton, "The Adirondacks: A Political History."
19. Found at: http://digitalcollections.archives.nysed.gov/index.php/Detail/Object/Show/object_id/14460.
20. Malmsheimer, Bentley and Floyd, "Conserving the Northern Forest."

21. Dobbs and Ober, *The Northern Forest.*
22. Ibid.
23. J. Collins, "A Sustainable Resource for a Sustainable Rural Economy," in *The Future of the Northern Forest*, ed. C. Klyza and S. Trombulak (Middlebury, VT: Middlebury College Press, 1994).
24. Reidel, "Endgame for the Northern Forest."
25. Northern Forest Lands Council, "Finding Common Ground.
26. Johnson, Stewart and Mockrin, *Demographic Change in the Northern Forest.*
27. Ibid.
28. E. Thorndike, "Envisioning the Future of Wilderness."
29. G. Chilson, "Hope for the CABR?." The status of the CABR remains murky. The website for the UNESCO Man and the Biosphere Programme (MAB) in 2020 listed three administrative authorities for the CABR: the APA, the U.S. Forest Service (USFS) and the Vermont Agency for Natural Resources (VANR). When phone calls were attempted in 2020, UNESCO MAB's designated CABR phone contacts for the USFS and the VANR appeared to be obsolete. A subsequent conversation with a representative of the APA indicated that the APA "hasn't been involved with the CABR in over a decade." A group calling itself the Champlain Adirondack Biosphere Network (CABN) claims to "carry out the strategic goals" of the CABR (https://champlainvalleynhp.org/heritage/champlain-adirondack-biosphere-reserve). The APA representative stated that he "was not aware of the CABN."

Chapter 4

30. A. Godine, "Hard Times Come Again No More," *Adirondack Life* (December 2000), http://www.adirondacklifemag.com.
31. Jenkins, *Adirondack Atlas.*
32. Balagtas, "The Low-Profile Poor."
33. Terrie, "North Country Needs Jobs."
34. Shaw, "The Caretakers."
35. John B. Trevor Jr. was commodore of the St. Regis Yacht Club in the Adirondacks during the World War II years and founding trustee of the Trudeau Institute. He was a director of the Pioneer Fund from 1959 to 2000 (web.archive.org/web/20121130130929/http://www.pioneerfund.org/Founders.html). The organization was reported to have had ties to eugenics and the study of human differences (see: G. Lichtenstein, "Fund Backs Controversial Study of 'Racial Betterment.'" *New York Times*, December 11, 1977; D. Nelkin and M. Michaels, "Biological Categories and Border Controls: The Revival of Eugenics in Anti-immigration Rhetoric," *International Journal of Sociology and Social Policy* 18, no.

5/6 [1998]: 35–63; P. Lombardo, "'The American Breed': Nazi Eugenics and the Origins of the Pioneer Fund," *Albany Law Review* 66 [2002]: 209; Tucker, *The Funding of Scientific Racism*).

36. Cox, Woods, Holmes, Porter and Erickson, "Survey of Public Priorities as a Guide for Sustainable Investment Strategies."
37. Davies, "The Economic Importance and Wood Flows."
38. Egan, "Characteristics of New York's Logging Businesses."

Chapter 5

39. Collins, "The Adirondack Park."
40. Gore and Lapping, "Environmental Quality and Social Equality."
41. Erickson, "In Search of Sustainable Development," 261–80.
42. Van Riper, Manning and Reigner, "Perceived Impacts of Outdoor Recreation."
43. Shoumatoff, "The Real Adirondacks."
44. Kalinowski, "Will Climate Change Mean More Wind?"
45. Craig, "Warming Climate Affects the Adirondacks in Many Ways."
46. Ibid.
47. Egan, "Transitioning from Forest Restoration Welfare to Sustainable Forest Health: Wildfire Season."

Chapter 6

48. Shoumatoff, "The Real Adirondacks," 336–46.

BIBLIOGRAPHY

Abello, T. "Forest Protection Bill Stalled in Congress." *Adirondack Daily Enterprise*, September 30, 1997.

Abruzzi, W. "Conservancy May Sell Some Finch Land Parcels to Be Able to Buy the Rest." *Adirondack Daily Enterprise*, August 3, 2007, 1, 7.

Adamic, L. "Aliens and Alien-Baiters." *Harper's Monthly Magazine* 173 (June/November 1936).

Adirondack Almanack. "2014 Tourism Study: Hiking, Paddling, Water Sports Big Draws." November 15, 2015.

Adirondack Daily Enterprise. "The Adirondack National Park Report Summarized." August 1, 1967.

———. "Ad'k Council to Discuss Climate Change." September 18, 2002.

———. "Against Biosphere Reserve Designation." July 15, 1993.

———. "Another Agency Enters the Olympics Picture." March 31, 1977.

———. "Anti-prison Group Started in Gabriels." July 28, 1981.

———. "Bill Roden on National Park." August 9, 1967.

———. "Conservancy Buys 161k Acres." June 19, 2007.

———. "Finch, Pryn [*sic*] Co. Executive Discusses Industry's Viewpoint on National Park." September 19, 1967.

———. "Life" (editorial). August 23, 1967.

———. "A Look at Forest Job-Loss Numbers." August 24, 1993, 1.

———. "Maybe We Should Do Other Things Than Hike." June 14, 2018.

———. "Residents Gather to Save Fire Tower." August 5, 2004.

———. "Text of Laurance Rockefeller's Speech." October 30, 1967.

———. "U.S., Canadian Educators Meet to Plan Biosphere Educational Curriculae." May 19, 1990.

Adirondack News. "Millionaires Object." December 29, 1906.

———. "Private Park Fishing." May 28, 1904.
———. "Supporting Fires Caused by Agencies Not Related to Logging." May 23, 1903.
———. December 27, 1902, 5.
———. July 9, 1904, 5.
———. July 13, 1907, 1.
Adirondack Park Regional Assessment Project. Executive Summary. May 2009.
Alexander, J., and J. Davenport. "Adirondack Park Population Totals Under Scrutiny." *Post-Star* (Glens Falls, NY), April 19, 2011.
Anich, M. "Fulton County Opposes State's Land Purchases." *Adirondack Daily Enterprise*, October 17, 2012.
The Association for the Protection of the Adirondacks. *Seventy-Second Annual Report*. Schenectady, New York, June 1973.
Bagstad, K., and M. Ceroni. "The Genuine Progress Indicator: A New Measure of Economic Development in the Northern Forest." *Adirondack Journal of Environmental Studies* 15, no. 1 (2008).
Balagtas, A. "The Low-Profile Poor." *Glens Falls Post-Star*, July 31, 1988.
Boyer-Rechlin, N. "Prison Opposition." *Adirondack Daily Enterprise*, August 24, 1981.
Briere, S. "Report: Younger People Needed in Adirondacks." *Adirondack Daily Enterprise*, February 20, 2021.
Brooklyn Daily Eagle. December 3, 1870.
———. January 9, 1871
———. March 8, 1871.
———. September 17, 1873.
———. January 23, 1874.
———. April 11, 1874.
———. September 7, 1879.
———. December 1884.
———. November 22, 1885.
Bruinius, H. *Better for All the World*. New York: Alfred A. Knopf, 2006.
Burton, H. The Adirondacks: a political history. *Lake Placid News*, December 14, 1978.
Calkins, A. "Adirondacks Boast Fair Share of Ghost Towns." *Plattsburgh Press Republican*, October 29, 1989.
Cerbone, A. "Gorgeous Day Saw 'Probably the Highest Use in High Peaks History.'" *Adirondack Daily Enterprise*, September 28, 2020.
———. "Jones Says Selling Camp Gabriels Is a Priority." *Adirondack Daily Enterprise*, May 15, 2018.
Chilson, G. "Hope for the CABR?" *Adirondack Journal of Environmental Studies* 13, no. 2 (2006).

Christian, N. "North Elba Journal; Recalling Timbuctoo, a Slice of Black History." *New York Times*, February 19, 2002.

Collier, J. "Coping with Population Decline." *Adirondack Daily Enterprise*, April 23, 2011.

Commercial Advisor (Potsdam), February 15, 1893, 3.

Collins, J. "The Adirondack Park: How a Green Line Approach Works." In *The Future of the Northern Forest*, edited by C. Klyza and S. Trombulak. Hanover, NH: Middlebury College Press. Published by University Press of New England, 1994.

Commission on the Adirondacks in the Twenty-First Century. *The Adirondack Park in the Twenty-First Century*. Vol. 2. Albany: State of New York, April 1990.

Conroy, T. "'Forever Wild' Significant." *Press-Republican*, May 23, 1985.

Courier and Freeman (Potsdam, NY). June 7, 1882.

———. September 29, 1926.

Cox, G., A. Woods, T. Holmes, W. Porter and J. Erickson. "Survey of Public Priorities as a Guide for Sustainable Investment Strategies in the Four Northern Forest States." *Adirondack Journal of Environmental Studies* 16 (2010): 15–23.

Craig, G. "Warming Climate Affects the Adirondacks in Many Ways." *Adirondack Daily Enterprise*, October 20, 2018.

Crocker, A. "Seventy-Ninth Annual Report." Association for the Protection of the Adirondacks. August 1980.

Crowley, P. "Hiker Shuttle Follows Federal Funds to Wilmington." *Adirondack Daily Enterprise*, September 7–8, 2019.

———. "No New Land for Now." *Adirondack Daily Enterprise*, February 14, 2011.

———. "An OK Compromise, but Then What?" (editorial). *Adirondack Daily Enterprise*, August 9, 2012.

Crowley, P., and G. Kelly. "Some Local Leaders Encourage 14-Day Quarantine for Visitors." *Adirondack Daily Enterprise*, March 25, 2020.

Daily Journal (Ogdensburg). April 24, 1874.

———. August 16, 1875.

———. November 1, 1878.

———. September 1, 1879.

———. April 10, 1883.

———. May 15, 1886.

———. October 11, 1886.

———. August 22, 1894.

———. September 28, 1905.

Davies, R. *The Economic Importance and Wood Flows from New York's Forests*. Concord, NH: North East State Foresters Association, 2007.

Delaware Gazette (Delaware County, NY). November 20, 1878.

Dobbs, D., and R. Ober. *The Northern Forest*. White River Junction, VT: Chelsea Green Publishing, 1995.

Donaldson, A. *A History of the Adirondacks*. New York: The Century Company, 1921.

Duquette, J. "Adirondack Pied Piper." *Adirondack Daily Enterprise*, June 2, 1987.

———. "From Verplanck Colvin to Nelson Rockefeller, the Progression of the Adirondack Park." *Adirondack Daily Enterprise*, June 10, 1989.

———. "The Good Life of the Camp Caretaker." *Adirondack Daily Enterprise Weekender*, November 25, 1989.

———. "Verplanck Colvin Remembered." *Adirondack Daily Enterprise*, March 5, 1988.

Egan, A. "Characteristics of New York's Logging Businesses and Logging Business Owners." *Northern Journal of Applied Forestry* 26, no. 3 (2009): 106–10.

———. "The Collaborative Forest Restoration Program: Lessons Learned and Implications for CFLRP." *Ecological Restoration* 32, no. 1 (2014): 13–15.

———. *Haywire: The Unraveling of Maine's Forest Industry*. Amherst: University of Massachusetts Press, forthcoming.

———. "Transitioning from Forest Restoration Welfare to Sustainable Forest Health: Connecting the Dots on New Mexico's Most Catastrophic Wildfire Season." *Journal of Forestry* 110, no. 4 (2012): 229–30.

Elizabethtown Post. "Verplanck Colvin of Adirondack Survey Fame Dead." June 3, 1920.

———. February 11, 1904.

Erickson, J. "In Search of Sustainable Development: Lessons in Application from the Adirondack Park." In *Sustainability in Action*, edited by J. Köhn, J. Gowdy and J. van der Straaten, 261–80. Northampton, MA: Edward Elger Publishing, 2001.

Essex County Republican, October 23, 1873.

———. April 23, 1874.

Evening Gazette. March 3, 1891.

Evening Post. "Two on a Vacation in the Adirondacks." January 12, 1918.

Fernow, B. "Timber as a Crop." In *Proceedings of the American Forestry Association at the Tenth, Eleventh and Twelfth Annual Meetings, Washington, December 1891, 1892, and 1893*. World's Fair Congress, October 18 and 19, 1893. Volume X. Washington, D.C., 1894.

Forest and Stream. 1882. "Adirondack Survey Notes." https://archive.org/stream/ForeststreamXIX#page/162/mode/2up/search/Adirondack+Murray.

———. "Game Law Amendments." November 23, 1882.

———. "New York Game Laws." January 18, 1883.

———. "A Query." January 25, 1896.

Forest, Fish and Game Commission of the State of New York. *Seventh Annual Report of the Forest, Fish and Game Commission*. Albany: Forest, Fish and Game Commission of the State of New York, 1902.

Fox, W. *First Annual Report of the Forest Commission for the Year 1894*. Albany: Forest Commission of the State of New York, 1895.

———. "Forestry Matters in New York." In *Proceedings of the American Forestry Association at the Tenth, Eleventh and Twelfth Annual mMetings, Washington, December 1891, 1892, and 1893*. World's Fair Congress, October 18 and 19, 1893. Vol. X. Washington, D.C., 1894.

———. *New York Fisheries, Game, and Forest Commission, Fourth Annual Report, 1898*. Albany: Wynkoop, Hallenbeck, Crawford, January 20, 1899.

———. *Second Annual Report of the Forest Commission for the Year 1895*. Albany: Forest Commission of the State of New York, 1895.

Gloversville Daily Leader. "New York Canadian Pacific, Second Hearing on Project for a Big New Railroad." October 4, 1902.

Gore, P., and M. Lapping. "Environmental Quality and Social Equality: Wilderness Preservation in a Depressed Region, New York State's Adirondacks." *American Journal of Economics and Sociology* 35, no. 4 (1976): 349–59.

Goren, J., S. Coppola and N. Woodworth. "Summits Overrun over Labor Day." *Adirondack Daily Enterprise*, September 10, 2016.

Hadley, B. "Camp Gabriels to Close within a Year." *Lake Placid News*, January 18, 2008.

Halper, L. "'A Rich Man's Paradise': Constitutional Preservation of New York State's Adirondack Forest, a Centenary Consideration." *Ecology Law Quarterly* (1992).

Hammond, S. *Hunting Adventures in the Northern Wilds*. New York: Derby and Jackson, 1858.

———. *Wild Northern Scenes or Sporting Adventure with the Rifle and Rod*. New York: Derby and Jackson, 1857.

Hari, J. "The Wrong Kind of Green." *Nation*, March 22, 2010.

Haverty, N. "Cuomo: 'Reducing the Madness of an Incarceration Society.'" North Country Public Radio, 2014

Headley, J.T. *The Adirondack: or, Life in the Woods*. New York: Charles Scribner, 1849

———. *Letters from the Backwoods and the Adirondac*. New York: John S. Taylor, 1850.

Hoffman, C.F. *Wild Scenes in the Forest and Prairie*. New York: William H. Collier, 1838.

Iszler, M.. "In Adirondacks, DEC Forest Rangers Ask for More Boots on the Ground." *Albany Times Union*, November 24, 2017.

Ithaca Daily Journal. October 26, 1878.

———. September 6, 1879.

———. December 8, 1880.

Izzo, E. *Adirondack Daily Enterprise*, March 26, 2020.

———. "State Begins Route 73 Roadside Parking Ban." *Adirondack Daily Enterprise*, May 29, 2019.

Jackson, J.P. Science for Segregation: Race, Law, and the Case against Brown v. Board of Education. New York: New York University Press, 2005.

Jenkins, J. *The Adirondack Atlas*. Syracuse, NY: Syracuse University Press and the Adirondack Museum, 2004.

———. *Climate Change in the Adirondacks: The Pathway to Sustainability*. Ithaca, NY: Comstock Publishing, a division of Cornell University Press, 2010.

Johnson, A. "Adirondack Heroes Colvin and Murray." *Lake Placid News*, December 12, 1985.

Johnson, K., S. Stewart and M. Mockrin. *Demographic Change in the Northern Forest*. Issue Brief No. 46. March 20, 2012. Concord: Carey Institute, University of New Hampshire, March 20, 2012. Accessed October 11, 2015. http://carsey.unh.edu.

Kalinowski, T. "Will Climate Change Mean More Wind?" *Adirondack Almanack*, January 2, 2012. The LA Group. "The Adirondack Park: Seeking Balance." *Adirondack Park Regional Assessment, 2014*. Saratoga Springs, NY: The LA Group, 2014.

Knight, C. "Governor Goes Out with Adirondack Land Deal." *Adirondack Daily Enterprise*, December 31, 2010.

———. "Is It Time to Charge a Fee to Use the High Peaks?" *Adirondack Daily Enterprise*, 2016.

———. "State Will Close 4 Prisons, Including Chateaugay (second update)." *Adirondack Daily Enterprise*, July 26, 2013.

L.A. Group, P.C. Adirondack Park Regional Assessment Project. May 2009.

Lake Placid News. "Adirondack Battles Were Front-Page News in Those Days." August 12, 1927.

———. "Adirondack Murray Did Much to Popularize the Adirondacks." October 8, 1926.

———. "Approves Forest Amendment: Trustees of the Association for the Protection of Adirondacks Go on Record for Constitutional Changes." October 22, 1915.

———. "In Congress: The Northern Forest Stewardship Act." December 22, 1995.

———. "No Permits for High Peaks Trails." September 10, 2020.

———. "Our Public Forests." August 13, 1915, 4.

———. "T. Morris Longstreth Writes of Club Guide." July 10, 1925.

Levine, J. "Study Finds High Peaks Parking Areas Often Overflow." *Adirondack Daily Enterprise*, June 6, 2018.

———. "Thousands of Hikers Out on Labor Day Weekend." *Adirondack Daily Enterprise*, September 4, 2019, 1.

Lewis County (NY) Democrat. January 26, 1881.

Lichtenstein, G. "Fund Backs Controversial Study of 'Racial Betterment.'" *New York Times*, February 26, 2006.

Loeb, J. "Conservation: Then and Now." *Adirondack Daily Enterprise*, August 30, 1967.

Longstreth, T.M. *The Adirondacks*. New York: Century Company, 1917.

Loope, P.F. "The Adirondack League Club." *Adirondack Daily Enterprise*, June 20, 1955.

Lynch, M. "Adirondack Council Says Review Board Oversteps." *Adirondack Daily Enterprise*, February 4, 2011.

———. "Controlling Crowds in the High Peaks." *Adirondack Explorer*, July 14, 2017.

———. "Local Gov't Review Board Opposes State Land Purchases." *Adirondack Daily Enterprise*, February 2, 2011.

Lynch, M., and C. Morris. "Mixed Reaction to State Land Purchase." *Adirondack Daily Enterprise*, August 7, 2012.

Malmsheimer, R., W. Bentley and D. Floyd. "Conserving the Northern Forest." *Journal of Forestry*, April/May 2002.

Malone Palladium. 1869–79.

Mann, B. "Adirondack Tourism Lifts Some Boats." *Adirondack Almanack*, July 8, 2014.

———. "After Reorganization, Adirondack Nature Conservancy Chapter Has New Leader." North Country Public Radio, August 30, 2017.

———. "Do Big Adirondack Conservation Deals Hurt Loggers?" North Country Public Radio, October 1, 2012.

———. "How Prisons Became the North Country's Normal." North Country Public Radio, December 2, 2013.

———. "A Million Acres of Adirondack Timberland Becoming Junk." North Country Public Radio, February 14, 2013.

———. "North Country Prisons: Hard Times in Siberia." *Adirondack Almanac*, September 9, 2013.

Martin, M. "North Country Costs Studied." *Glens Falls Post-Star*, July 12, 1989.

Martine, M. "Solomon Blamed for Stall of the Northern Forest Act." *Adirondack Daily Enterprise*, September 28, 1996.

May, R.W. "Genetics and Subversion." *Nation*, May 14, 1960.

McLaughlin, B. "A Fascinating Glimpse at What Might Have Been." *Adirondack Daily Enterprise*, November 10, 1983.

McMartin, B. "The Adirondacks: It's Not a Model; It's a Mess." *Adirondack Journal of Environmental Studies* (Spring/Summer 1999).

———. *The Great Forest of the Adirondacks*. Utica, NY: North Country Books, 1994.

———. *Perspectives in the Adirondacks*. Syracuse, NY: Syracuse University Press, 2002.

Mills, K.. "World's Ecological Eyes Pointed to Adirondacks." *Glens Falls Post-Star*, April 28, 1989.

Morris, C. "State Reaches Deal to Buy 69,000 Acres." *Adirondack Daily Enterprise*, August 6, 2012.

Murray, W.H.H. *Address Delivered on the Sabbath Following the Assassination of President Lincoln in the Second Congregational Church*. New York: John F. Trow, Printer, 1865.

———. *Adventures in the Wilderness*. Boston: Cupples and Heard, 1869.

Nearing, B. "Graying of Adirondacks Presents Future Challenges." *Albany Times Union*, May 19, 2014.

———. "State: Adirondack Land Swap Would Save Jobs at Mine." Timesunion.com, May 16, 2013.

New York Fisheries, Game, and Forest Commission. *First Annual Report, 1895.* Albany: Wynkoop, Hallenbeck, Crawford, 1896.

———. *Second Annual Report, 1896.* Albany, NY: Wynkoop, Hallenbeck, Crawford, 1897.

———. *Third Annual Report, 1897.* Albany, NY: Wynkoop, Hallenbeck, Crawford, January 20, 1898.

New York Forest Commission. *Annual Report for 1891.* Albany, NY: James B. Lyon, 1892.

———. *Annual Report for the Year 1892.* Albany: New York State Forest Commission, March 30, 1893.

———. *First Annual Report for the Year 1885.* Albany: New York State Forest Commission, May 18, 1886.

———. *First Annual Report of the Forest Commission of the State of New York for the Year 1885.* Albany: New York State Forest Commission, 1986.

New York Forest, Fish and Game Commission. *Sixth Annual Report, 1901.* Albany, NY: Wynkoop, Hallenbeck, Crawford, 1902.

New York State Department of Labor. 2009. Accessed March 17. www.labor.state.ny.us.

New York Times. "To Preserve Adirondacks: Wealthy Owners of Estates in the Mountains Form an Association for This Purpose." June 21, 1902.

———. "Plan for the Adirondacks." January 4, 1971.

North East State Foresters Association. August 2007. Accessed March 17, 2009. www.nefainfo.org.

Northern Forest Lands Council. "Finding Common Ground—Conserving the Northern Forest." March 1994. https://nsrcforest.org.

———. *Tenth Anniversary Forum Final Report.* April 25, 2005.

Ogdensburg (NY) Journal. January 29, 1874.

———. April 17, 1874.

———. October 15, 1874.

———. November 7, 1890.

———. January 20, 1893.

———. January 15, 1886.

———. February 14, 1896.

On the Saint Lawrence and Clayton Independent. October 21, 1892.

Plattsburgh (NY) Daily Press. "Climates Change." September 25, 1894,

Plattsburgh (NY) Republican. May 21, 1887.

———. March 31, 1888.

Plattsburgh (NY) Sentinel. "The Adirondack Question." April 11, 1884.

———. June 4, 1880.

———. August 27, 1880.

———. June 30, 1882.

———. April 6, 1883.
———. October 9, 1885.
———. January 29, 1886.
———. February 20, 1891.
Randall, W. *North Creek News Enterprise*, March 18, 1942.
———. *North Creek News Enterprise*, March 29, 1967.
Rappaport, L. "Adirondack Panel Looks at Federal Role in Park." *Adirondack Daily Enterprise*, August 7, 1988.
———. "Protest Today at APA." *Adirondack Daily Enterprise*, July 16, 1990.
———. "UN Taps Region as Reserve." *Adirondack Daily Enterprise*, May 1, 1989.
Reidel, C. "Endgame for the Northern Forest." *American Forests*, March/April, 1993.
Rielly, K. "The Sustainable Tourism Equation." *Adirondack Almanack*, November 27, 2012.
Ringlee, R.J. "Statement of Position on the July 27, 1967 Proposal for an Adirondack Mountains National Park." Adirondack Mountain Club Inc. October 30, 1967.
Robinson, N. *Environmental Regulation of Real Property*. Vol. 1. New York: Law Journal Press, 1982, 6: 22–3.
Rockefeller, L. "The Adirondacks and the Future." An address before the Adirondack Mountain Club. Warrensburg, New York. October 28, 1967.
Rosenzweig, C. *Responding to Climate Change in New York State: The ClimAID Integrated Assessment for Effective Climate Change Adaptation*. Synthesis Report. Albany: New York State Energy Research and Development Authority, 2011.
Russell, M. "Debate Rages after UN Designates Adirondacks a 'Biosphere Reserve'." *Adirondack Daily Enterprise*, July 9, 1993.
Seggos, B. "125 Years of the Adirondack Park." *Adirondack Daily Enterprise*, May 30, 2017.
Shaw, C. "The Caretakers." *Adirondack Life*, December 1988.
Shea, K. "Adirondack Schools Confront Woes, Worries and Wants." *Adirondack Daily Enterprise*. August 28, 2017.
Shoumatoff, A. "The Real Adirondacks." In *Rooted in Rock: New Adirondack Writing*, edited by J. Gould. Syracuse, NY: Syracuse University Press, 2001, 336–46.
State of New York Conservation Department. *The Adirondacks: New York's Forest Preserve and a Proposed National Park*. Albany: State of New York, 1968.
St. Lawrence Herald. 1893. January 20, 1893.
Stransenback, E. "Rain Lessens Danger of Adirondack Forest Fires." *Press Republican*, August 3, 1983, 17.
Sun (New York). June 18, 1876.
_____. August 6, 1879.
_____. November 6, 1880.
_____. September 28, 1887.
_____. February 4, 1891.

Suter, H.M. "Forest Fires in the Adirondacks in 1903." Bureau of Forestry Circular No. 26. 1903.

Terrie, P. *Contested Terrain*. 2nd ed. Syracuse, NY: Syracuse University Press, 2008.

———. "North Country Needs Jobs." TimesUnion.com. August 3, 2014.

Thomson, L. "An Address before the Albany Institute on the Adirondack Wilderness." March 18. Albany, NY: Weed, Parsons & Company, 1884.

Thorndike, E. "Envisioning the Future of Wilderness." In *The Great Experiment in Conservation—Voices from the Adirondack Park*, edited by W. Porter, et al. Syracuse, NY: Syracuse University Press, 2009.

Trombulak, S., and R. Wolfson. "Twentieth Century Climate Change in New England and New York." *Geophysical Research Letters* 31 (2004).

Tucker, W.H. *The Funding of Scientific Racism: Wickliffe Draper and the Pioneer Fund.* Champaign: University of Illinois Press, *2007.*

Vance J. "Adirondack Industries." *Plattsburgh Sentinel*, February 22, 1895.

Van Riper, C., R. Manning and N. Reigner. "Perceived Impacts of Outdoor Recreation on the Summit of Cascade Mountain, New York." *Adirondack Journal of Environmental Studies* 16 (2010).

Vrooman, D. "Regional Land Use Controls in the Adirondack Park." *American Journal of Economics and Sociology* 34, no. 1 (1975): 95–102.

Wallace, J. "Massena Pellet Mill at the Forefront of Renewable Energy Industry." North Country Public Radio, July 11, 2012.

Warren, J. John. "An Open Letter to Brian Mann." *Adirondack Almanack*, August 9, 2011.

Watertown (NY) Re-Union. "The Black River and Its Sources." March 9, 1876.

White, W. "Chapter III Ad'k Century." *Adirondack Daily Enterprise*, February 22, 1956.

Williams, D. "Adirondack Harry: A Friend of Wilderness Guides." *Adirondack Daily Enterprise*. December 24, 1994.

———. "Colvin Reports Again." *Adirondack Daily Enterprise*, December 16, 2006.

Wynn, G. "Deplorably Dark and Demoralized Lumberers: Rhetoric and Reality in Early 19th Century New Brunswick." *Journal of Forest History* (October 1980): 168–87.

Young, E. *Special Report on Immigration*. Forty-Second Congress, 1st sess. Executive Document 1. Washington, D.C.: Government Printing Office, 1871.

ABOUT THE AUTHOR

Andrew Egan has been a tenured professor on the forest science faculties of the University of Maine and Laval University (Québec). He has been dean of the School of Forestry and Natural Resources at Paul Smith's College, executive director of the New Mexico Forest and Watershed Restoration Institute, dean of the Faculty of Science at Brandon University and head of campus in the University of Maine system.

Egan has worked internationally, including as a Peace Corps volunteer with the Forestry Training Institute in Liberia and with the Department of Environmental Science at Central Luzon State University in the Philippines; and during seven USAID-sponsored visits to the Dominican Republic on projects related to forestry and community development. During his career in higher education, he has been awarded two Fulbright Scholarships to teach and conduct research at the Institute of Forestry in Nepal. He is cofounder of The Gola Foundation, which supports the education of disadvantaged youth in rural West Africa.

Egan is the author of over one hundred scientific and technical papers and of the forthcoming book *Haywire* (University of Massachusetts Press), about the unraveling of Maine's forest industry. His research has focused on the interactions among forest operations, silviculture and the forest environment, woods labor in the forestry sector of the northern forest region and the socioeconomic and ecological dimensions of forest and watershed restoration.

Visit us at
www.historypress.com